MW00478379

CORNBREAD RED

POOL'S GREATEST MONEY PLAYER

BOB HENNING

BEBOB

CORNBREAD RED

POOL'S GREATEST MONEY PLAYER

BY BOB HENNING

Published by: **Bebob Publishing**
P.O. Box 530411
Livonia, MI 48153

First Printing 1995

Printed in the United States of America

Library of Congress Catalog Card Number: 95-094819

ISBN 1-887956-34-4 $14.95 Softcover

Cover design by Patrict Powers
Cover photo by Chuck Looney

Acknowledgement

Many people deserve thanks for their contribution to the creation of this book. At the top of that list is my wife, Kathy, whom I thank for her undying support and tireless proofreading. Special thanks go to Billy Joe and Bernetta Burge for their countless hours of interviews and willingness to open their lives to me.

In addition, I offer a respectful thank-you to all the pool players and lovers of the game who have shared memories and insights with me. May the game we love continue to be appreciated.

Individuals I wish to specifically thank are: Barb Henning, John Sanitate, Roy Kosmalsky, Harry Sexton, Thomas Wheelis, Dorothy Wilson, Steve Lomako, Wade Crane, Danny Beile, George Loridas, Beryl Gobbard, John McCue, Catherine Goddard, Susan Binkley, Vicki Paski, George Middleditch, Conrad Burkman, Milt Hardin, Jesse Nikon, Jay Helfert, Larry Otto, and the Mecham family.

Cornbread and Bernie dedicate their contribution to this work to their children and grandchildren: Sandy, Greg, Randy, and Stefanie Nicole.

Author's Note

This work is based on the true life of Billy Joe Burge. Built on the bones of truth, the imagination of the author, and the creative memories of others, this book is intended to be read as a biographical story. All characters are considered to be fictitious and any similarity to persons, living or deceased, with the exception of those who have given permission to use their names, is purely coincidental.

"I love life—and I hope she loves me, too."

Bill Tyler 1977

Preface

In 1986, the award-winning movie, "The Color of Money," hit theater screens across the nation. When Paul Newman, playing Fast Eddie Felson, uttered the triumphant words "I'm back!," the beauty and color of the game caught and held the attention of millions. The popularity of pocket billiards sky-rocketed. Within two years, upscale billiard rooms were opening up like dandelions in springtime. Everywhere. Japan—Hong Kong—New York—Europe.

Professional Tours were organized and picked up by television. A World Federation was formed and Championships were held. For the first time, tournament purses and product endorsements were sufficient to support a full field of gifted and talented professionals. Pool had arrived as *the game of the nineties*.

It had made a long, circuitous trip from its heyday of the 1920's. Tuxedos and over stuffed parlors had fallen away to the seedy images of the depression and the preoccupation of the war and post-war periods. A brief revival came in the sixties when Fast Eddie made his debut in the movie, "The Hustler," but it didn't last. For the next twenty years, world-class pool limped along—kept alive by a handful of devoted survivors.

This is the story of one of those men—one of those men who gave their lives to the game—who kept it alive while Eddie Felson was gone. This is a story of heart and wit; of gambling and confrontation. This is a story of the greatest *money* player ever born—the one they call the *Living Legend*—Cornbread Red.

1

FULTON

"No, Billy Joe, that's not the way it was at all," Ila Maurine said. She was a large woman, or so most people thought, until they got close enough to realize that what they thought was large, was really just compact strength. Her pleasant face was framed with bright, red hair, pulled back from her forehead in a gentle wave and curled under on the sides. "Taylor Burge was never meant to be your real name. Taylor is my maiden name and Burge is your Pap's last name. The doctor who came when you were born was drunk and put the wrong names on the birth certificate. Your real name is Billy Joe Burge."

The boy looked up at her. "You look just like that lady in the war bond poster, Mom," he said, as she dabbed at the corners of his face with a wet cloth.

She pushed a few unruly locks of red hair, lighter than her own, away from his blue eyes and smiled. "That's a sweet thing to say, honey. I want you to give that same beautiful smile to the photographer when he tells you to."

"Okay, Mom, I will," the boy said, and he meant it too. This had been a *good* week. Trains loaded with fresh, young recruits going off to the war had come through Fulton each of the last three days. The trains stopped to pick up the local passengers, but the soldiers were not allowed to get off. Billy Joe had gone down to the depot with his friend, Tommie Smith, to watch them go by. They were waving at the soldiers when one of the men noticed the candy machine against the far wall of the building. "Hey, boy! Run and get me one of those candy bars," he yelled, flipping a nickel through the open window. When Billy Joe got the candy and threw it back to him, the man tossed another nickel out and told him to keep it. It started a stampede. Hungry soldiers were clamoring for Mars Bars, Snickers, and Fifth Avenues. They were hanging out of the windows, each one trying to be heard above the others before the train pulled out. The boys ran in a frenzy—buying for a nickel—selling for a dime. They emptied the candy machine, for the second time, just this morning.

And now this—the very thought of having his photograph taken made him shiver with excitement. Ila Maurine was so happy with the money he gave her, she was taking him, and only him, to Jack Grady's barber shop for his first *store bought* hair cut and then to the five-and-ten where the local photographer had his tiny booth.

A photograph was practically a grown-up thing. He didn't know of any other ten-year-old boy in Fulton having gotten one yet—not if you didn't count the rich kids. And, by golly, he wanted to be grown-up, coming and going as he pleased—laughing and cussing when he wanted to. Just like Pap. At the thought of his father, Billy Joe flinched. He hadn't seen or heard from Miller in almost a year now. Not since the last time he was out drunk for a week and spent all the money. Maurine had cursed him and refused to open the door when he came home and demanded something to eat. She cried afterwards—a lot.

"Come on, son. Let's go," Maurine called from the screen door.

Billy Joe jumped to his feet and thrust both hands into his pockets. They were full of coins he had kept for himself. He was surprised to feel how warm they were.

The city of Fulton, in 1942, was a busy place. As a railroad junction, the rushing and pulsing of the great war build-up was visible, but for the most part, just passing through to somewhere else. Most of the town's able-bodied men had answered their country's call and joined that flow to distant places, leaving the town in the hands of the well entrenched, the old, the women, and the scoundrels.

Main Street ran through the center of town and was the border between Kentucky and Tennessee. The city of Fulton, Kentucky, was on the north side, and South Fulton, Tennessee, was on the south. When the area was known only to the Indians, not one single tribe claimed it. It was a no man's land—low and mosquito ridden. They called it the Dying Ground. Later, during the Civil War, Main Street was the dividing line between loyalties and ideologies and the area became a dying ground for another race. Even today, Billy Joe knew, as he walked on the Tennessee side with his mother, it made a difference which side of the street you came from. He didn't understand *why* he was supposed to be proud for being from Kentucky, but according to Maurine, he was.

All he knew was that he was glad to be going to Jack Grady's barber shop. Jack Grady was one of the few adults in town who called him Red. He would say things like: "How ya doing there, Red—or—What's cookin', Red?" He was friendly and personable, always clean and wearing black, shiny shoes. Billy Joe liked him.

Six or seven storefronts before the barber shop Red stopped like he always did when he walked by Three-Way Billiards, one of the two pool halls in Fulton. He grabbed the concrete window sill with both hands, pulled himself up on his tiptoes, and pressed his face to the glass.

Inside the poolroom were several pool tables and a row of men drinking beer at the small counter. At the table closest to the window a man smacked the cue ball into a rack and the balls moved around the table, bouncing off the rails and colliding into each other. There were red ones and green ones, purple ones and blue ones. A solid black one went around the table twice and landed in the far corner pocket. Red was fascinated. Pap had taken him in there a couple years ago and the men had set him up on an RC Cola case and let him knock the balls around. It was great.

"Billy Joe!" Maurine shouted. She was about a hundred feet down the side walk. He dropped down from his tiptoes and ran to catch up.

◆   ◆   ◆

The war years were good for Ila Maurine and her children: Jimmy, Billy Joe, Bobby, and her little girl, Olladine. She got work at the ammunition plant in Mylar, Tennessee, and the regular paycheck was a godsend. Jimmy and Billy Joe also managed to bring home small amounts of money. It was the first time, in a long time, that the family wasn't living day to day. She did her best to keep a short rein on the boys, but with working and without a man around, it was hard to do. Bobby minded pretty good—Jimmy got into an occasional scrap or two—but Billy Joe was turning into more than she could handle.

"You got a regular hero there, Mrs. Burge," Jack Grady said one July day when she ran into him in town.

"What do you mean?" she asked.

"They got your redhead over there at Three-Way Billiards. He's about on his third soda pop by now, I guess."

Maurine looked puzzled.

"Now don't be getting worried, ma'am," Jack said, holding a hand up. "He's not in any trouble or anything. In fact, if it wasn't for your boy, it's a darn good chance Bruce's nephew would 'a died down there at the creek."

Maurine's hand flew to her mouth. "What?"

"Yessirree, they were swimming in one of those deep pools. Bruce's nephew dove in and cut himself real bad— your boy said it was on an 'ole rusty tub sunk in the mud. Anyhow, your boy pulled him out and carried him on his back up the hill until he found some grown-ups. Bruce is so happy, I'm surprised he ain't tried to buy the kid a beer yet. Hahaha."

"Oh, Lord," Maurine cried, pushing her way past the man and hurrying down the street. When she got to the poolroom she looked through the dirty window and saw Billy Joe and a small group of men gathered around the counter and the far table. Her boy was standing on a wooden crate, a cue stick in his hand, leaning over the green surface of the table. A pudgy man she recognized as C.P. Bruce, the owner, was helping him aim. At least two of the men were holding glasses of beer. One was Dick Stennen, a man with hair as red as her son's. She rapped on the glass.

Red looked up and dropped the stick on the table. Jumping off the crate, he turned his back to her and moved out of sight behind the owner. She rapped on the glass again—louder—and both son and owner turned and walked toward the front entrance. Maurine left the window and met them there.

The owner smiled at her. "Good day to you, Mrs. Bur—"

"I don't want my boy in there," she said sharply, cutting him off, "and I, for godsakes, don't want him drinking beer."

C. P. Bruce took a calming breath and bit his bottom lip. "Look here, Ma'am," he said, "I've done the best I can, and I haven't been able to keep him outa here. I throw him out the front and he comes in the back. I throw him out the back, he comes in the front. Besides, he deserves a little special treatment today."

"I heard all about it, Mr. Bruce, and I'll not have my boys going the way of their father."

C. P. nodded. "Look, Ma'am, just this morning he got Dorothy Stennen to call me out front here and both he and Barney snuck in the back. It's driving me crazy trying to keep him outa here. I don't know what else I can do."

Ila Maurine looked at him and then at her son. "Get on home, Billy Joe." She kept her eyes on him as he skipped down the sidewalk and disappeared around the corner. She turned a cold gaze back to C.P. Bruce. "You're encouraging him," she said.

C. P. looked at the sidewalk and shook his head. "No, Mrs. Burge, I'm not. I'm not," he said looking up, "but I wish I could."

Her anger was checked by his sincerity. "What do you mean, Mr. Bruce?"

"In all due respect, ma'am, I appreciate your concern. I see a lot of boys come through my poolroom, and I can see a lot of them will never amount to anything. Most of them, if they do manage to stay out of trouble, won't ever have anything to look forward to except to work someone else's land." He pulled a white handkerchief from his pocket and wiped the sweat from his forehead.

"Go on."

"Your boy's one of the most coordinated people I've ever met. He's got a natural talent for the game. Is it right to stand in the way of such a gift? What else is he gonna do? What else does he have to look forward to?"

She continued staring at him.

"Can you see him farming? Or keeping a store? How's he gonna make a livin', Mrs. Burge?"

"He'll learn a trade," she said, "that's why I've got him going to school."

"Come on, ma'am. The boy's skipping school at least half of the time—surely you must be aware of that?"

She ignored his question and remained silent, still looking at him. After a brief moment, a faint blush appeared on both cheeks and she nodded her head, almost imperceptibly. It was another moment before she spoke.

"I fear for him," she said in a low voice, "he's headstrong and hot-tempered. He doesn't know how to control himself, and I can see it's only a matter of time before he's openly defying me."

"That's exactly what I'm talking about," C.P. said. "He loves playing pool! He'll learn self-control if you let him. That's what playing good pool is all about!"

She looked surprised to see such passion from him. She took a few seconds to compose herself and then said, "Perhaps you're right, Mr. Bruce, what do you propose?"

"Write me a letter. Give Billy Joe permission to come in my room underage. I'll teach him everything I know and I'll do the best I can to keep him out of trouble."

After a moment, the tension in her face relaxed and she spoke with determination. "I'll write you that letter," she said, looking into his eyes, "but I expect you to keep my boy away from alcohol." She held her gaze for a few seconds and then abruptly turned and walked away.

C.P. Bruce was still nodding his head when she disappeared around the corner.

2

SHOES

Tommie Smith was angry about it. It wasn't fair that
Billy Joe had been going into the poolroom for over a
year already, and he still couldn't. They were the best of
friends, and had been for a long time, but this was too
much. He sure as hell wasn't gonna shine up to him like
some of the other kids were doing. Big deal—so what if
he could go and play pool with the grown-ups.

He kicked a stone lying in the middle of the dusty
road. He was tall for his age; slender and blond. He was
on his way to meet Billy Joe and some of the other kids in
town at Smith's Cafe. It was Saturday—nothing special
about it—not really. Nothing to do except hang out, listen
to the juke box, and joke around. What made him mad
was that in his mind, he could already hear Billy Joe
Burge saying, "Well, fellas, I got to be going, there's
supposed to be a big game over at Three-Way Billiards."

He wasn't mad at his friend, though. He'd be bragging
himself if he could, and he enjoyed the stories Billy Joe
could tell. He wasn't mad at C.P. Bruce, either. It was
C.P. who was keeping him out of the poolroom, but it was
something he had to do, and Tommie understood that. The
truth was, he didn't know who to be mad at—he didn't
know *who* made the rules, but he knew—it wasn't fair.

◆   ◆   ◆

Billy Joe missed his friends. He loved going into the poolroom and he enjoyed the company and attention of the older guys who came in there, but he missed the easy fraternity of kids his own age. Sometimes, he wished he could be in two places at once. Places where things were happening. *Action.* That's what C.P. called it. "You like the *action*," he had said, "you like the excitement—the gambling."

When he got to Smith's Cafe, his friends were already there. Tommie and Melvin Smith were at the juke box and gave him a wave of greeting. Paul and Barney Stennen were sitting at one of the tables with their sister, Dorothy, and another brown-haired girl.

"Hey, Billy," Barney called out. Both Stennen boys were tall and wiry, with black hair and dark eyes. Barney was loud and boisterous. Paul was quiet and thoughtful. Billy Joe walked over and joined them at the table.

"Did you win any money today?" asked Dorothy. The girl beside her giggled.

"Heck, I ain't even played any pool yet today," he replied. "But I almost always win when I do."

Tommie and Melvin came over from the juke box. "Did you see Paul's new shoes?" Tommie asked. Paul stuck a foot out from under the table. It was shod in shiny, black leather.

"Where'd you get those?" Billy Joe asked.

"My mother bought 'em."

Billy Joe looked again. New shoes were hard to come by, you had to have the money and the war stickers. He looked at his own beat-up loafers.

"Maybe if you win enough money playing pool, you can get some, too," Tommie said. The others echoed him.

"Hey, let's get out of here and go somewhere," Barney said, changing the subject.

"Where?" one of them asked. There was silence, all of them searching for an idea.

Barney was the first to speak. "Let's hitchhike to Mayville," he said.

Out on Main Street, they walked as a group toward Mayville, about twelve miles away. Whenever a car would come by, all five boys would stick out their thumbs.

"Hey," Paul said, after several cars passed by, "nobodies gonna pick up a bunch of guys like us. Let's put the girls out in front—maybe they can get a ride."

The girls moved to the edge of the blacktop and, with coaxing from the boys, stuck their thumbs out at the next few cars. None stopped. With further encouragement and laughter, they tried flagging the cars over with sweeping arm motions. When that failed, Dorothy's friend bared her right leg to the knee, and turned it seductively.

The third vehicle, a truck, pulled over.

"Girls in the front—boys in the back," the driver yelled above the noise of the engine. The boys piled in the back of the open truck. It was filled with straw and crates of produce. The girls got in the front and the truck lumbered back onto the highway toward Mayville.

In the back of the truck, the boys discovered oranges, grapefruits, and lemons—all scarce in the wartime economy. By the time they arrived in Mayville, a crate was forced open and while the girls thanked the driver for the lift, all five boys jumped from the back with lemons in their pockets.

Mayville was the same as Fulton—nothing much to do there, either. They ended up at the local diner, playing the juke box with their last nickels and sharing a plate of french fries. Without the owner noticing, Billy Joe and Paul cut up the lemons, and with the help of the girls and the sugar on the table, made lemonade for all of them. When the nickels and the lemonade were gone, they left the diner and walked toward the edge of town to thumb a ride back to Fulton.

"Hey, look at that," Barney said, pointing to a large, wooden bin sitting at the edge of the hardware store's parking lot. It was about as tall as a man, with the Good Will emblem and a large sign saying, "Help the Poor," on the side of it.

The kids went over and looked around. Billy Joe found a hinged window in one of the walls, and pulled it open. They took turns leaning through the opening and into the bin. It was full of clothing, kitchen utensils, old shoes, and other items.

"We should do our part to help the poor," Billy Joe said to the others.

"We are the poor!" Tommie yelled as he pulled a handful of clothing and a threadbare blanket out of the opening.

"No," Billy Joe stopped him, "this is for the people who don't have anything at all. For orphans and stuff."

"That's right," Paul said, "If you take anything out, you got to put something of your own back in for the poor people."

Dorothy spoke. "Let's all put something in."

They agreed and pulled clothes out of the bin and tried them on. Billy Joe found a ragged shirt that fit and traded it for the less ragged one he was wearing. Dorothy found a pair of socks and traded them for her own. Each of the others followed in turn. Paul went last.

"You better not do that," Dorothy said, when she saw the black, shiny shoes in his hand. "You'll get a whippin' for sure."

Paul shrugged his shoulders and dropped his new shoes through the opening and into the bin. He pulled a battered pair of work boots out, sat down, and put them on.

On the way back to Mayville, the kids were quiet. Billy Joe, try as he might, could not keep his eyes off the dirty boots on Paul's feet.

◆   ◆   ◆

The big news in town that summer, was the fight between Dick Stennen and Charlie Borders. Charlie, in his taxi, had raced through town, swerving back and forth, sliding around corners, and jumping curbs in an attempt to evade Dick, who was shooting at him from the open window of his Chevy. Dick, who worked up at Browder's

Mill, had come home to find Charlie in *his* house, with *his* wife.

To the men of Fulton, Dick Stennen was a gambling man who frequently lost and was easily angered—liable to do *anything* when hot. No one was surprised when he chased Charlie Borders down Main Street. No one was surprised when he went back home two days later—drunk—pulled his rifle out of the trunk of the Chevy—and shot his wife in the chest—right through the front door she had refused to open.

She surprised everyone and lived. Dick surprised everyone and killed a totally different man, from Clinton, in a senseless rage. The bloody murder scene was discovered by two boys on their way to school: Billy Joe Burge and Tommie Smith.

Later that summer, Billy Joe played a match against a man who owned a laundry in a nearby town. The men in Three-Way Billiards were happy to lay a few bucks on Billy Joe, and happier yet when he won. Jack Grady, who bet the heaviest, was the happiest. "You can't be shooting pool with that hair hanging in your eyes," he said to Billy Joe, "you come and see me and I'll take care of it—on the house."

Billy Joe meant to see him the next day, but went swimming with Tommie and some of the other kids instead. On a dare from Barney, he dove into the same swimming hole C.P. Bruce's nephew dove into a year

earlier, and suffered the same fate. After being laid up for
a week, at Maurine's insistence, he made it in to Jack's.

"Yessirree," Jack Grady said to the boy in his barber
chair. "If a man was on the run, this would be a good
place to start from. He could be standing in the middle of
Main Street with the law right behind him and jump all
the way to Tennessee in a single tremendous leap.
Hahaha."

The skinny boy in the chair looked at Jack Grady in
the small mirror on the wall. He was big and tall with
dark, black hair and huge hands. All the kids liked Jack
and Billy Joe felt special to have his full attention. It was
obvious that the barber liked him.

"He could be in Missouri in half an hour—Illinois and
Arkansas in an hour. Hell, if he had a car, he could be in
any of twelve states in time for dinner. Yessirree."

Red smiled. This was a familiar theme for Jack, and
one that Red enjoyed. He had first heard it when he was
ten and it still made him feel like he could go anywhere—
do anything.

Jack continued. "If a man had a boat, or hell, even a
good-sized log, he could get anywhere he wanted to. Float
right down to New Orleans and get one of those dancing
girls. Hahaha." He took the brush out of the soap mug and
dabbed lather around Billy's ears and the back of his
neck. "Yessirree, that would be the way to go. If he was
hard-headed, he could go upstream all the way to
Chicago, or even Montana if he wanted to—yessirree—a
man could get anywhere he wants from here."

"He could hop a freight car down at the ice factory," the boy volunteered as the barber stropped the razor on his leather strap.

"That's right, I practically forgot. This here's the banana capital of the world. Ain't a banana in the country get to where it's going without coming here first. A man could get in one of those cars and go anywhere." He inspected the edge of the razor and stropped it some more.

The front door swung open and a thin, black man entered the shop. It was Jess, the shoeshine man. He had a copy of the Saturday Evening Post in one hand and a bottle of soda in the other. He, too, was well liked by the kids and was one of the few Negroes who mixed easily with the white population. Most of Fulton's colored stayed in their own section and, as far as Billy Joe could tell, never did anything but have barbecues.

"Ain't you suppose' to be in school?" he said, sitting down in the chair reserved for customers.

"I cut my leg," the boy said, a faint blush rising to his face.

"That's right," Jack said. "You're looking at a real live hero here, Jess. Yessirree, when he couldn't find anyone to save, he jumped in the creek and had to save himself. Got cut on the same washtub the kid last year did."

"What you talkin' 'bout he saved himself? Billy Joe, you jumped in dat same creek?"

"I forgot it was in there," Billy Joe said. It sent chills up his spine just thinking about the huge gash the tub had put in his thigh. He felt pressure on his head as Jack held it still with one of his hands.

"Settle down there Billy Joe. Don't be jumping around while I got this razor here." He scraped at the lather and fuzz on the back of Red's neck. "Ain't you seen enough blood for one summer?"

3

FENCES

Thomas was a slim man, with dark hair and a hint of Indian in his face. He was a quiet man, easy to be with and easy to overlook. When they were called upon to remember him, most people only remembered the smoothness of his voice and the softness of his eyes. Today, he was sitting in a rocking chair on the small porch of the sharecrop house. He was deep in thought.

Few people knew him as he was in Europe. Behind the lines, Thomas and his comrades buried sound machines to pinpoint the German guns when they were fired. Once, they were playing cards on a blanket, when boom—boom—boom—the German guns zeroed in on them. They hit the ditches with the shrapnel flying. Another time, they were laying phone line when they came face to face with three German tanks. They ran like hell—machine gun fire right behind. Still, he was glad to have been in the service. He had a place to stay, most of the time, and plenty to eat and clothes to wear. Not like the depression years, and not like now, with its constant struggle to make ends meet. He was twenty-two when he, and hundreds of others, returned from the war.

Many of them found no work, not even farming. He got lucky and landed a job with the railroad. All that winter, he lowered little stoves full of sizzling charcoal through the tops and into the boxcars of bananas. When the warm weather came, they replaced the stoves with blocks of ice and lowered those through the rooftop doors. A little later, the foreman's brother came back from the navy and Thomas' job was gone.

Ila Maurine was there to console him. She was twelve years his senior and in the middle of a divorce. Her husband was gone at the time and no one really knew where. She told Thomas that even when Miller Burge was working at Browder's Mill, he was never around. He'd cash that paycheck and start to drink and wouldn't none of the family see any of it or any of him until it was all drunk up. Try as he might, Thomas was unable to stop himself from thinking poorly of Miller Burge. It wasn't the drinking—God knows he drank his own part in the service—and before too. He knew a guy up in the hills around Dukedom who used to make *fruit juice*. But how could a man walk away from a woman like Ila Maurine? She was such a strong woman, a really *good* woman. And those kids, too. Three boys and a little girl. He didn't understand it, but he was glad it was he, Thomas, sitting on the porch and not the other. The whole family had welcomed him into their lives and he was damn glad to be there. He had married her two weeks ago and moved the whole family out here to Kingston Stores to work this sharecrop. Now, one of the boys—fourteen-year-old Billy Joe—had disappeared.

Thomas knew right from the start that Billy Joe was different. He'd go with the others and walk Main Street on Saturday night, but he didn't end up at Smith's Cafe with them. He went to the poolroom and gambled with grown-ups—and he was good at it, too. He was bringing money home when no one else in the family was. God knows that was appreciated. With that thought, Thomas remembered the hoeing he had come out to do. He stood up, stretched, and walked out into the tobacco field.

Charlie Borders was on his way back from dropping off a fare in Dukedom, when he saw the Burge kid, the redheaded one, hitchhiking on the side of the highway. Charlie never gave a ride, for free, to anyone. "You got to pay to play," he was fond of saying. He made exceptions only when it was clearly to his advantage. This was such a time.

He'd been hearing stories about the kid. One was about him beating an old guy out of some money at Bruce's. When the man refused to pay, the kid had climbed up on the roof and hit the guy in the head with a piece of concrete when he came out. Knocked him flat.

By this time, Charlie had already gone a hundred feet or so past the kid. He hit the brakes and pulled over to the shoulder, raising a cloud of dust. Checking the mirror for traffic, he confirmed the clearance, and made a wide U-turn. He drove past the kid's surprised face and made another wide turn. He pulled up and waved the boy into the cab.

"I got no money, Charlie. I'm hitchhiking," Red said, as he opened the door.

Yeah, right, Charlie thought. Like I didn't hear you just won two-hundred off that asshole in Mt. Vernon. "Go ahead and get in, Billy Joe," he said, "I haven't seen a single car since I left Dukedom. You'll end up walking to town for sure."

Red got in the cab. He had a dirty, white shirt on, with both sleeves rolled above the elbows. All the buttons except the lowest one were unbuttoned. The part of his chest showing, like his face, was red from the sun and looked tender. The bib of his overalls was hanging loose at his waist. On his feet, he wore brown, battered penny loafers, covered with dust and barren of pennies.

"Where you heading, son?" Charlie asked.

"Into town. I got to get to Three-Way Billiards."

"Ain't gonna be anyone in there on a day like today." He leaned forward to look up at the sky—farmers only came in the poolrooms on Saturdays and when it rained.

"There's supposed to be a Pea Pool game going on," Red said.

"Maybe the heat will drive someone in."

"Maybe."

They approached a large tobacco field on the left. A half dozen Negroes were working it. One older woman was stooped over near the road.

"Man, I'd hate to be in them fields today," Charlie said as they drove by.

"I was."

"What happened?"

"Thomas put me and my brother, Bobby, out there to hoe tobacco. Bobby's still out there."

"And you?"

"Man, it's too hot for me. I threw that hoe down and jumped the fence. I can make more money in this Pea Pool game, than I could in a whole week in that field."

"Good thinking, son, real good thinking. A man's got to know when to take care of number one."

They rode in silence for several minutes.

As they approached Fulton, Charlie slowed the cab down. "Any time you want to make some real money, son, you come and talk to me."

"What do you mean?" Red asked.

"I'm talking about gambling," Charlie answered. "You can't always know when you're gonna win, but you can always know when you're gonna lose." He looked at the boy's face for his reaction. "When I make a bet, I aim to win it. When a man helps me, I make sure he gets what's coming to him."

Red looked at the grown man. The unspoken point was clear. Charlie was asking if he would throw a game— take a *dive*, as C.P. called it. He didn't know what to say. Charlie made it sound so normal. Then he remembered Jack and C.P. and the others who bet on him. No. It wasn't right. They were his friends. Then he remembered Dick Stennen and the dead man by the bridge. He felt fear and was glad when the cab pulled over to the curb.

"Think about it," Charlie said as Red got out.

"I will," Red answered. He slammed the door and silently vowed to never talk to Charlie again.

◆   ◆   ◆

"Those boys are gonna put me in an early grave yet," Ila Maurine said one evening a few days later. She was making pie crust, her small hands white with flour. There was a white streak in her red hair at the temple where she had pushed it back from her eyes.

"Everything's gonna be fine, Maurine," Thomas said as he sat in a chair at the table, watching his wife.

She gave the dough one last turn with the fork, took the damp lump out of the bowl, and set it on the lightly dusted table top. "I'd go get that boy with my hickory switch if I thought it would do any good." She cut the dough into three pieces and began to roll one of them.

"He's a good boy, Maurine. He don't hardly ever get in trouble and he don't ever sass or swear in front of you."

"He thinks his shit don't stink."

Thomas nodded. She was right. Billy Joe was a cocky, young guy.

She positioned the flattened dough over a pie tin and began pressing the edge between her fingers. "The way he struts around town with his shirt unbuttoned all the way down to his drawers, you'd think he had hair on his chest or something."

Thomas laughed. "He's just trying to impress the girls."

"Come on, Thomas, he don't hardly ever pay attention to girls. He's just plain, overall arrogant." She put the final flourish on the first crust and reached for the second.

"You know, Thomas, that boy hasn't been the same since he cracked his head open."

"He cracked his head open?"

"Yes, about three or four years ago. It was the fourth of July and the Baptist church took the kids to Reelfoot Lake for a picnic." She looked up at Thomas.

He knew the place. It was a large lake just across the state line. People said it had been made by an earthquake, when the Mississippi River jumped its bed.

"They had all these kids in a flat bed truck with those wooden sides on it," she continued, "and one of his fool friends was climbing up on the side boards, and Billy Joe thought he'd be a big show off and get up there after the other kid got down. Well, wouldn't you know it, the truck went by a tree and hit him right in the head with a big limb. Knocked him right off the truck."

Thomas whistled.

"The worst part was there were so many people on that truck, no one saw him get knocked off and no one noticed he was missing. If it wasn't for a soldier and his girlfriend who came by, he'd a died out there. You wouldn't believe what it did to his head, Thomas. There was gravel embedded in his scalp and everything. They said at the hospital that there was even gravel touching his brain. The poor boy, I couldn't get him to go to Sunday School after that. He just wouldn't go after he fell off that truck and no one missed him." She sat down at the table. "I'm worried about him Thomas, he hasn't been home for five days."

"You want I should go look for him, Maurine?"

"I wish you would."

Thomas got up and put his hat on. "I might be able to find him," he said. "But even if I drag him back here, I can't make him stay if he don't have a mind to."

"I know."

The screen door slammed as Thomas went out. Ila Maurine sat for a moment, let out a sigh, and got up to roll the remaining dough.

Thomas went to the poolroom on Lake Street. Red wasn't there and the three young guys playing Pea Pool hadn't seen him. "Why don't you try the park?" one of them suggested. Thomas crossed the highway to the park. There was a hard, smooth place there in the woods where people played craps. Red had won some money there just last week. When Thomas got there, the mosquitoes were terrible and no one was there.

He went to the hobo jungle. The last time Maurine had taken the switch to Billy Joe was when he was caught hanging around there. Since then, a railroad goon Thomas knew had talked to him about Red and the Stennen boys. He said they were breaking seals on the freight cars and stealing bananas and watermelons. Red was lucky he hadn't been caught or he'd have had his head cracked open again.

In the jungle, two hobos were cooking pork and beans in a coffee can and relaxed when they realized he wasn't a railroad guard. They, too, had not seen a redhaired boy.

He went by Smith's Cafe. Not there.

He went to C.P. Bruce's poolroom. As he opened the back door, he heard angry voices and what sounded like pool sticks being knocked off the rack and onto the floor. Recognizing Red's voice, Thomas stepped quickly into the dim interior of the room to see Billy Joe being chased by an older teenager. Red saw Thomas at the same instant and yelled at his attacker. "Boy, here comes my Daddy!"

Thomas stepped to the side and Red got behind him. The angry teen stopped, his way blocked. "What are you after him for?" Thomas demanded.

"He won all my money."

"Well, that's too damn bad—you had no business playing him."

"He tricked me—"

Thomas moved forward, forcing the young man between two tables and toward the front door. "Go on. Get the hell outa' here!" He reached down and picked up one of the cue sticks that lay scattered on the floor. The younger man hesitated at the door.

"White trash!" he screamed, giving them the finger. He bolted through the open door and slammed it. He was running when he passed the small window in the wall of the poolroom.

Thomas moved over to the cue rack and put the cue up. He reached down and picked up two others from the floor and put them on the rack, too. Red moved over to the small counter and Thomas joined him there. Red lit a cigarette and offered the pack.

"You want a beer?" he asked.

Thomas nodded. "All right."

Red motioned to the boy behind the counter. "Give Thomas a beer and give me one of them moon pies and an RC." Red paid and took his change over to the juke box while Thomas sipped his beer. The sounds of 'Mable on the Hill' filled the poolroom.

"Your mother's worried about you," Thomas said, when Red sat down.

"I'm all right."

"She wants you to come home."

"I can't come back home, Thomas. I'm making money here."

"No one's ever tried to stop you from playing pool, Billy Joe."

"I know that, Thomas. It's just too hard to get in here if I'm out on a farm somewhere. Besides, Bruce is letting me stay upstairs."

Thomas was silent.

"Look," Red said. He showed Thomas a few crumpled dollar bills. "Give these to Ma."

Thomas hesitated.

"Go on. Take it," Red said. "I can get more."

Thomas stuffed the bills into his pocket.

4

OAKLAND DON

By the time Tommie and the rest of the boys were allowed in the poolroom, Billy Joe already had a reputation. It was getting harder and harder to find anyone who would play him for money at either Lake Street or Three-Way Billiards. This was the second time he had hitchhiked to the city of Clinton to play a guy there. He had lost this time and fumed the entire way back to Fulton. He was on his way to Jack Grady's to borrow money when he saw Tommie Smith coming from the south side of town. Tommie yelled when he saw Red and waved frantically for him to stay where he was. Red waited at the corner for him.

Tommie ran up, catching his breath. He was excited. "Billy," he said, grabbing at Red's sleeve, "there's a guy in town—a pool player. Man, he's good. He's kicking the shit out of C. P."

"Is he still there?"

"They were playing Nine-Ball when I left. I've been looking for you for an hour."

"Let's go."

In five minutes they were on the Tennessee side of Main Street and coming through the door of Three-Way Billiards. A group of eight or nine men were sitting and

standing around the table closest to the counter. All eyes
were on C.P. Bruce who was stretching to reach the cue
ball three-quarters of the way down the table. Red and
Tommie moved quietly to the edge of the spectators as he
pushed it toward the four-ball which was by the long rail a
diamond and a half from the pocket. The balls hit funny
and the four rolled into the mouth of the pocket and
jawed. Bruce swore under his breath, clenched his mouth
in a tight grimace, and sat down.

A short, kinky-haired guy stepped out of the group of
spectators and walked slowly to the table. He was dark—
probably Italian—Red guessed. He chalked his cue as he
looked at the balls and without further hesitation sank the
five, six, seven, eight, and nine. All the balls were
pocketed with the same speed and as far as Red could tell,
he never used English or did anything fancy. Red was
impressed and moved through the ring of men to the
adjoining table and leaned against it. Tommie moved
beside him and whispered in his ear. "Charlie says his
name is Oakland Don and he's one of the top ten road
players in the country. But for godsakes don't tell anyone
else or Charlie will bust my ass. They're betting big
money on him and don't want no one to know. He's
giving C.P. the eight."

Red nodded. In Nine-Ball, both players had to shoot
the lowest numbered ball on the table first. The first to
make the nine-ball itself, on a legal hit, won. C.P. was
receiving a *spot* from the stranger. He could win by
pocketing either the eight or the nine.

Red watched as C.P. handed the stranger a ten-dollar bill which the dark-haired man folded neatly and put in his pocket. As C.P. moved to the foot of the table, Red kept his eyes on the stranger. He appeared calm, almost serene, as he waited to break. He was looking around the room with an easy movement of his head. Damn, Red thought, he thinks he owns the place. The man's eyes settled on Red and were held there until C.P. slammed the wooden rack onto its hook and said, "Break 'em." The man got down to break and Red looked at his hands. They were smooth-skinned and clean—not the hands of a farmer.

C.P. Bruce and the stranger traded ten-dollar bills back and forth as the men betting on the side whooped and moaned. Red watched in silence. After two hours C.P., who was doing the bulk of the giving, threw his cue on the table and said, "I can't play you like this, you gotta give me the seven."

"Okay, let's take a break," the darkheaded man said as he leaned his cue against the wall. "Come on, I'll buy you a beer."

The two men moved toward the small counter. C.P. looked at Red and motioned him over.

Red said good-bye to Tommie and joined the two men at the counter just as the stranger took a long pull on his Black Label, wiped his mouth with the back of his hand, and set the bottle on the counter.

"This here's the boy I told you about," Bruce said. "He's our local boy wonder. Billy Joe, say hello to Oakland Don."

"You shoot good," Red said as he shook hands.

"Pure luck." Oakland Don raised his eyebrows in mock disbelief and dropped them back down. "Bruce tells me he's taught you everything he knows. Says you're beating everybody's ass around these parts."

"I hold my own."

"That's good," Don smiled, "that's real good."

There was a moment of silence as the young man and the hustler stared at each other. It was broken by Don. "Our friend here is offering to stake me for some action in Arkansas and Missouri. Maybe even Illinois. He's suggesting I take you along. Are you up to it?"

The excitement of the idea rushed into Red's chest, filled it, and moved up to his head. He felt dizzy and had to bite his lip to stop from yelling out. C.P. Bruce mistook his silence as hesitation and spoke with encouragement. "You should do this, Billy Joe, you really should. This man can teach you things not another twenty-five guys in the world can."

Red nodded his head. "Okay," he said.

"All right!" Don smacked the counter with his empty beer bottle. "Today's Tuesday. Let me play a couple of these local guys and we'll leave on Thursday. Bring some extra clothes and don't forget your cue."

Red nodded again. His control had slipped and a happy grin had found its way to his face. The two grown men noticed and grinned themselves.

That Friday, they were riding in Don's black 1946 Plymouth. They had just left the small Arkansas town of

Blytheville and were on their way to Jonesboro. They had played in Blytheville, but it had not gone the way it was planned. Don had named Red "The Paducah Kid," and had bragged about him to the dusty farmers and other beer drinkers in the local bar. He was acting loud and drunk and in a short time had arranged an Eight-Ball match with two of them eager to take some money from a boy and a fool.

The plan was for Don to continue his act—weaving back and forth, miscueing, and otherwise annoying the competition—while at the same time moving the balls into position for Red to run out. Red was excited to play his role, but unfortunately, did not pull it off. It seemed as if he could not make a ball. The two Blytheville boys were hooting with delight at his attempts. Red got angry, and the angrier he got, the worse he shot. Finally, the 'inebriated' Don was forced to sober up to save their stake money.

"Boy, people in these parts sure do cool off quick," Don said. He glanced at Red who was sitting morosely in the passenger seat. "One moment they're acting all friendly and everything and the next moment they're downright mean and inhospitable."

Red's head dropped a little lower and he turned and looked out the window. He was on the verge of tears and was doing his best to hide it from Don. He clutched his cue case between his knees.

Don continued to drive. "We'll be in Jonesboro in about an hour. You want to talk about what happened?"

"I hate it."

"Well, that's good."

"I mean it. I can't stand it. I hate this game."

"You got to learn how to play it, Red."

"I can play the damn game, Don, and I can beat those two pricks, too." He hit the dashboard with the heel of his hand.

"Well, I suspect you can," Don said slowly. "Would you like to take a look at what happened so you don't have to go through it again?"

"Yes."

Don waited for him to continue.

"Well," Red searched for the words. "I wanted to win. I wanted to play good. And then, damn, I don't know what happened, Don, I really don't. I can't believe I missed that three in the side. I ain't never missed a shot like that in my life."

"You weren't with it."

"Yes, I was. I aimed that shot good, Don. I did. You know I did."

"You *buried* yourself in it. You knew it was important and you worried it to death. You got to have a little trust, Red, a little faith."

"I hate pool."

Don was quiet for a moment and then spoke. "Knock off the crap, Red. The beauty of this game is that it doesn't matter how you feel about it. The ball either goes in or it doesn't. You either win the game, or you don't. You either bust the other guy or he busts you. Period."

Red turned his head and stared out the window again.

"And another thing," Don continued. "This game *is* reality. When you miss, something *real* happened. There's no magic in it. When you get to know everything that's happening in a shot, you'll see what I'm talking about."

"I still don't know why I missed that three."

"Look Red, when we get to Jonesboro, I'm gonna drop you off at the poolroom. Get a table in back and practice. Don't be concerned with making the balls, just pay attention to what you're doing when you do. Can you handle that?"

"Yes," Red nodded, "I can."

Don pulled the car to a stop at an intersection. He pointed to a short road sign almost hidden by the weeds. It said Jonesboro—10 miles. He waited for a passing truck and then crossed the blacktop. "One other thing," he said as the car accelerated. "Don't look too good, or you'll blow our action for tonight."

Red smiled with relief.

The moon was full and bright when they left the poolroom later that night. It was brighter outside than it had been inside. Their shoes crunched on the gravel as they walked to the Plymouth where it was partially hidden in the shadows at the edge of the parking lot. Don was ecstatic. He stopped Red at the back of the car and put a hand on his shoulder. "That was beautiful!" he said. He held the thick roll of bills up to Red's face and laughed deeply. "Look at it! Look at it! Look at it! You did fine my young friend. Very fine." He slapped him on the back.

The fifteen-year-old boy's eyes were bright, his face flushed. He was swaying back and forth on the balls of his feet. "I did good, didn't I, Don?"

"I'm proud of you, Billy Joe." Don put the roll of bills back into his pocket. "They tried to put the pressure on and you didn't buckle. You just kept whacking those balls in the pockets. You should have seen the look on his backer's face when you cut that six-ball in," Don laughed. "I thought for a moment we weren't gonna get paid—he looked so sick. I thought maybe he didn't have the cash."

"How much did we get, Don?"

"I haven't counted it yet, but I know we won enough that we probably shouldn't be standing out here in the dark." He turned his head to look around the parking lot. They could hear the muted sounds of the jukebox playing in the pool hall. "The way that guy kicked that waste can—" Don paused. "Well—maybe he's a little too upset about losing."

Red felt a chill in his gut. "Ya know," he said, looking at Don, "he was talking to two guys in the corner when we were leaving."

Don pulled out his keys. "Come on," he said, "let's get out of here and get something to eat."

"I'm starved," Red said. He took another look around the deserted parking lot and walked to the passenger door. He put his hand on the chrome handle, and looked up to see Don at the drivers door still fumbling with the keys. As Don stepped back to open the door, his face moved into the moonlight. Red could not see his body, still hidden by the car and the shadows. My God, Red thought, it looks like—he caught his breath as a mental image surged forward from the past. The hair on the back of his neck rose and he shivered as the night breeze touched the exposed sweat. His grip on the door handle tightened as the force of the image rocked him.

He was on his way to school with Tommie Smith, when they found it. People said later that Barney Stennen's uncle and some other men had been shooting craps in the woods that Sunday. He and Tommie had found it on Monday. They had found it at the edge of the concrete bridge over the highway. Right there at the bridge's end. Barney's uncle had got into it with a guy and had cut his head off.

Red shivered again and realized the muffled voice he heard was Don yelling at him from inside the car.

Don pushed the passenger door open and yelled again. "Come on, Red! I wanna get out of here!"

Red got in and slammed the door. He rolled the window down as the car moved across the gravel and onto the blacktop. I did it, he thought, as the car accelerated. I really did it. He turned the vent window so that the cool air hit him full in the face. He leaned back and closed his eyes.

5

CHARLIE

Red stayed on the road with Don for the rest of that year and part of the next. They would go off for a couple of weeks and then return to Fulton. Most of the time they came back with more money than they left with. C.P. Bruce, still in for a piece of the action, was happy as hell.

Thomas and Ila Maurine, now at a different sharecrop, were also happy to see them. Red would show up unexpectedly with cans of lard, sugar, and flour. He'd come home with live chickens, and Maurine would pick 'em and fix 'em. The few times he showed up busted, he still helped. He was learning to wheel and deal—*making a game*—Don called it—to get what he wanted. He obtained the necessities the family needed by dealing with the local shopkeepers and others who wanted to bet on him.

When off the road, he would hang out at Three-Way Billiards where it was practically impossible for either he or Don to find a money game. After a few days of inaction, they would be forced back out on the road. It was after one such trip that Don gave him the news.

"I got a letter from home, Billy Joe. My brother bought a little poolroom there and my family wants me to come back and run it with him."

"You gonna do it?"

"Yeah, I think so. I've been on the road so doggoned long even my mind is tired. Besides, we're too well known around here. Everybody's heard about *the dago and the redhead.*"

Red felt uncomfortable and looked at the floor. Don noticed and understood.

"If you came with me," he said to the teenager, "you'd be known in a week and wouldn't get another game. You might as well stay here with your family."

Red nodded.

Don put a hand on his shoulder. "You've got ability, kid. You've got heart. You still don't have much pool sense," he smiled, "but you'll learn." He gave the boy's shoulder a squeeze.

"Hey, I know how to take that money down."

"Yes, you do. But don't be one of those guys who get stuck on the cash, Billy Joe. The game is more than that."

"I know."

"And another thing. You won't be able to stay around here forever. Not if you want to bring your game up. You have to find the better players."

"How can I win if I'm playing guys who are better than me?" Red asked.

"You've got to decide what you want, Billy Joe. If it's just the money—that's easy. Just don't play anyone who can beat you."

"I like the money."

"If you want to be a great player, however, that's another thing. You can't get good playing traps all the time. You have to match up."

"I wanna be great," Red said.

"Make up your mind. You wanna be rich or you wanna be a pool player?"

"I want both."

"Well, you better get good then. Get to where you can walk into a room—look around—and know you're the best. I don't mean *think* you're the best, I mean where you *know* you're the best." He looked at Red. "If you do that, you never have to worry about having money—just find a poolroom. Okay?"

"Okay," Red said.

"All you got to worry about then, is finding a game."

They laughed.

◆   ◆   ◆

In the two weeks since Don left in the Plymouth, Red had gotten only one worthwhile game. He played the local photographer one afternoon for ten dollars a set. The photographer, who was *getting two games on the wire*, could not believe that Red could win five games before he won three. Red, who could do this easily, followed Don's advice and won two, lost one, won two, lost one—all afternoon long. The photographer stayed in the game until he'd lost all his money, a grand total of over sixty dollars. When he still wouldn't quit, Red put the sixty dollars up against the man's little photo booth and won that, too.

"Keep your stand and just owe me the sixty," Red said to the dismayed photographer. "Maybe we can play some more later."

After the man agreed and left the poolroom, Red stayed on the table and practiced his Pea Pool break. In Pea Pool, each of the players had to shake a numbered *pill* out of a bottle. His pill, which he would promptly hide in his pocket, would determine the ball he would have to make to win. If he made one of the other player's balls, that player would be out. All the balls were shot in order from the lowest to the highest and any made on the break counted. Most players, when they got the break, would smash the balls and hope to make one. Don had taught him to go for his own. He'd gotten where he could make any ball in the rack, on call, about ten-percent of the time.

He was practicing for about ten minutes, when C.P. Bruce came over to the table. "Got you a game, Billy Joe," he said.

"Great," Red said as he propelled the cue ball toward the rack. "Who is it?"

"Some guy from Evansville. Charlie and a couple of his friends are bringing him in."

Red made a face as he watched the table. The ball he intended to make had collided with another and ended up in the center of the table. "When?"

"Saturday. They want to play for big stakes, Billy."

"How much?" Red asked.

"Leave that to me and the other guys, you just play your best."

"Okay." He liked being free from worrying about the money. "What's the game?"

"One-Pocket."

Saturday night was Red's favorite time in the poolroom. It was always crowded and noisy. Usually there was more action on Saturday than all the rest of the week put together. Red particularly liked Saturday nights when there was a big match going down—especially if he was in it. He liked being the center of attention. He liked being surrounded by excited people putting bets down—making and calling last minute challenges before the game began. Tonight was such a night.

He was nervous when he first arrived. He liked One-Pocket, but didn't have a lot of experience with it. Don had taught him the basics, and said he was a natural at it. It was a game of *moves*—a lot of defense and complex strategies. It wasn't like Nine-Ball where you shot the balls off as quick as you could. Don had said there was level upon level in One-Pocket—a man could spend his whole life learning to put eight balls in his own pocket before the other guy put eight in his. Red was nervous because it was a hustler's game—easy for a person to play without revealing his true ability.

Red could tell by the excitement of the bettors that C.P. wasn't kidding. There was going to be a lot of money changing hands over this match. He saw Charlie Borders and avoided him by walking over to C.P., Jack, and the other men who were betting on him.

Once the game started, Red calmed down. Don had told him that the best way to judge the skill level of an opponent in One-Pocket was to watch his speed control. If a player seems to be missing, but his ball always ends up close to his pocket when he misses, he could be *stalling—*

playing below his real ability. This guy was really missing and he was missing often enough that Red was certain he could beat him.

He became more certain as the match developed. The more certain he became of the outcome, the more confident he became. The more confident he became, the stronger he played. Finally, in the second to last game, Red paused from his table run to enjoy the moment. He was totally in control of the situation. He knew what to do and how to do it. There was no way anyone could stop him. This was his moment. He looked around the room. It seemed as if time was standing still. He noticed Charlie watching him from the corner of the room. There was an intense look on his face and when he realized he had Billy Joe's attention, he motioned downward with his thumb. Red did not respond. He turned back to the table and looked again at the lay of the balls. The clarity that was present just a second ago had faded. He felt anger kindle in his stomach. The image of Charlie motioning was still with him. "When you start to lose it," he remembered Don telling him, "pick up the pace—get out in front of your thoughts. Get moving and stay with the shot."

He picked up the pace, shot the three-ball in with authority, and quickly followed with the others. As he stood up from the table, he could hear Jack and C.P. above the cheers of the others. He would be glad to win the next game and get this match over. He waved at his friends and looked around the crowd while he waited for the other player to rack. Charlie was no longer in sight.

"I gotta take a break," his opponent said and walked towards the back of the room where the john was. Red set his cue on the table and joined Jack and C.P. at the counter.

"You're doing fine, Billy," Jack said, handing him a cold RC.

Red took the soda. "I played the right moves in that game. I wish Don was here to see it."

"You did the right thing when you banked his six-ball out of there, I thought for sure you'd go for your own."

"No way. Don taught me that move. Don't ever bank your own ball when you can bank his."

C.P. laughed. "You didn't know it when you played that kid from Clinton last month. Cost me five dollars."

"I know it now." Red watched his opponent come out of the john and head back toward the table. "I got to pee," he said to Jack, "keep an eye on my cue."

In the restroom, Red threw some water on his face and looked in the mirror. His nerves were acting up again, but not a single sign of it showed on his exterior. Satisfied with his inspection, he picked up the dirty bar of soap. He was looking down, washing his hands, when he heard the bathroom door close, and saw the black shoes behind him.

"What the fuck you doing?" a loud voice said.

Red looked up at the mirror. It was Charlie.

"Charlie—" he turned, backing up against the sink.

"What the fuck you doing, Burge?"

"I'm just playing pool, Charlie—"

"You better wake up and get with the program!"

"Come on, Charlie, I'm playing for Jack and C.P.," Red tried to explain.

"I don't give a fuck who you're playing for. I've got a lot of money on this game and no piece of white trash is gonna fuck me out of it." Charlie took a step closer.

Red held his hands up and tried to move to the left.

"You dump when I tell you to!" Charlie shouted. He put his finger in Billy Joe's face. "You dump the goddamn game!"

"No!" Red yelled. "I'm not gonna do it."

Charlie moved to block the path to the door, his finger still in Red's face, his mouth an ugly snarl.

Just then the door swung open. It was one of the men who was betting on the game. His face was flushed—drunk. "Sorry," he said, "didn't know it was occupied." He tried to turn, lost his balance, and lurched in between Red and Charlie. Red squeezed through the opening and into the poolroom.

He was halfway across the room before he realized how fast he was moving. He forced himself to slow down. He saw both C.P. and Jack look at him in surprise and watched their expressions change as they realized what had happened. Both of them stood up.

Red went directly to the table. As he picked up his cue, he realized the fear was gone. In its place was a cold, hard fury. He broke the balls—made one in his corner, and left himself with an easy shot. With absolute certainty, he began his run-out.

6

JAIL

Thomas' favorite crop was tobacco—it required care and attention, and it, more than any other, allowed him to feel productive. He had planted the seeds in long wooden boxes and covered them with canvas. As soon as the plants were a couple of inches high, he would gently remove each one from the box, and plant it in the field. He was out checking the progress of these starter plants when Jack Grady drove up in his old Ford.

"Hey, Thomas," he said, leaning his head out the window. "They got your boy over at Hickman in the county jail. You better get over there."

Thomas came around the fence and up to the car. "What happened?" he asked.

"I don't know the whole story, Thomas. Some friend of Charlie's accused them of stealing tires or something like that. Just between you and me, though, a kid can't go around beating all the big shots out of money without pissing someone off. They arrested him over in South Fulton and you know how they are there."

Thomas nodded. The cops on the Tennessee side of town had a reputation for being mean. It was common rumor that if a man went to jail there and had a few dollars on him, he wouldn't have it when he got out.

"They arrested him with that Paul Stennen—I thought somebody ought to let you know."

"Thanks, Jack."

◆ ◆ ◆

The Fulton County Jail, in the town of Hickman, was a small jail. Besides Red and Paul, there were only two other prisoners. When the bond was set at five-hundred dollars apiece, both of them were resigned to a long stay. Much to their surprise, Paul was called before the judge the next day.

"What happened to my friend?" Red asked the jailer when Paul failed to return.

"The witness never showed up. The judge dropped the charges and sent him home."

"What about me?"

"That's up to the judge," the jailer said.

The days dragged into weeks, and the monotony was punctuated only by Ila Maurine's Tuesday afternoon visits. She would bring fried chicken, banana pudding, cabbage, and other home cooked delights. Red could not find out why he was still in jail, how long he would remain, or what he could do to get out.

He was bored. He shared his Tuesday meals with the jailer and played poker with him whenever there were no other prisoners. Once, when a young car thief from Paducah was in for a few days, Red got his first tattoo. It was a crude skull and crossbones, made by hand with Indian Ink and a needle. He was lying on his bunk admiring it, late one evening, when he was interrupted by the jailer.

"I got a surprise for you," the jailer said.

"What?"

"I'm gonna let someone in to see you."

"No kidding," Red said, sitting up, "who is it?"

"You just wait, and I'll bring 'em in."

It was Tommie.

"How ya doing, Red?" he asked from the other side of the bars.

Red jumped off the bunk and greeted his friend at the cell door. "Tommie! It's good to see you." He stuck a hand through the bars and his friend clasped it.

"You all right, Red?"

"No. I'm not. I gotta get out of here, Tommie, I'm goin' stir crazy."

"Yeah, well when you get out, you better keep going."

"Keep going? What are you talking about?"

"Man, you don't even know what's going on, do you?"

"Tell me, goddamn it."

"Man, the judge is in with Charlie."

Red sat back down on the bunk. It made sense.

"You should come with me," Tommie said. "I'm going with the carnival when they leave town next week."

"You're going with the carnival?"

"Yeah. I've got a job running a game on the midway. I'm gonna be on my own—do as I please."

"Where are you going?"

"Memphis. We're supposed to hit a whole bunch of little towns on the way. Supposed to be there in three weeks."

Red gave it some thought. "Tommie," he said, "You've got to talk to C.P. and Jack for me. See what they can do to get me out of here. If you see Charlie, tell him I'm leaving town with you if I get out of here."

"All right, Red," Tommie said, "I'll do what I can."

7

SKILLO

The owner was a fast talker; quick to twist the truth and bend the rules. He started them on the straight games—the balloon joint, where the customer threw darts at balloons pinned to the wall, and the basket joint, where customers threw balls into a basket. Red discovered a talent for calling people in. He would pick individuals out of the crowd and yell at them as they walked by. He learned to challenge them, shame them, entice them— whatever it took to get them to come over and take a shot at his game. The louder and bolder he was, the more they played.

The carnival took the place of Red's family. It was a loose and easy group—high on acceptance and low on instruction. Red and Tommie's wild behavior was tolerated, and even respected. Their days were filled with money, booze, fights, laughter, and the constant stream of faces coming down the midway. Whenever the action died in one town, the whole show would pack up and move to another.

It was after one of these moves that they discovered the big joints—Razzle, Skillo, and Pinstore. These were the illegal gambling games that opened on the midway when the coast was clear, and folded when the cops were near. They went and watched whenever they could. It was fast, dangerous, and exciting.

"Maybe you can run one of these joints some day," the owner said. "If you've got the balls."

"We ain't afraid of nothin'," the boys replied.

"Free tickets! Free tickets!" Red yelled. He was set up near the entrance of the midway—with the first shot at the locals coming in. He was relaxed. The owner had a guy who "paid the laws off" and that relieved some of the pressure. He and Tommie had left their first show in Kansas City because of the *heat.* They had simply looked in "Billboard Magazine," found a show playing where they wanted to go, and left. Once a carny had learned the big games, and could take the pressure, he was welcome anywhere.

The key to this game, Red thought, as he watched the crowd, was picking the customers. He singled out a middle-aged man in the crowd. "Free tickets!" he yelled, but the guy walked on by. Red scanned the crowd again and saw two rough looking guys coming down the midway. He kept quiet until they, too, passed by. He and Tommie had both gotten into fights running this game.

Red's voice had developed a hoarse quality. He didn't know whether it was from the cigarettes, the booze, or the yelling, but he liked the sound of it. "Free tickets!" he yelled at a pasty faced guy in his late twenties. "Five points for free, get to ten—win the money! Right here—win the money!"

The mark stopped and looked at the chart. In Razzle, the customer threw six marbles out of a cup and onto a board with numbered holes. The numbers of each throw were added up and that number had a certain value in points as specified on the chart. Some of the numbers were blank, others were worth from one-half point on up to two points. There were a lot of blanks around the mid-thirties.

"How do you play?" the guy asked.

"Throw these balls out. We add up the numbers and you get what's on the chart. If you get ten points you win."

"I'll give it a try," he said.

Red handed him the cup which he swirled once and dumped onto the board. "Here we go," Red said, starting the count, "4, 12, 18, 20, 22, and 4 makes 26." He pointed to the chart, 26 was worth two points. "Two points and your five free points is a total of seven points. You need three points to win."

The man took more change out of his pocket and gave it to Red.

"Throw 'em," Red said, handing over the cup. The man took it and threw again.

"5, 10, 18, 24, and the last two balls, 32 and 7 is 39. Check 39." He looked at the chart, knowing the other man's eyes were going there too. Thirty-nine was worth one and one-half points. "That's a total of eight and one-half points."

The man paid and threw again. One of the balls fell into a hole marked Jackpot.

"Here we go," Red said. "7, 12, 18, 22, and the last two—24 and 5 is 29. Check 29."

The chart showed one point for 29, giving the mark a total of nine and one-half.

"What's that Jackpot thing mean?" the man asked.

"You can take a shot at the jackpot if you want," Red said, pulling a wad of cash out from under the counter. "It costs five dollars a throw."

The man looked at the pile of money, now resting at the edge of the game board. There was at least a hundred dollars there. He looked up at the chart, down at the game board, hesitated for a split second, and then pulled a five out of his pocket and gave it to Red. He tried it three more times before giving up and moving down the midway. Red directed his attention back to people walking by. "Free tickets!" he yelled.

It was impossible in this game to throw anything but blanks. No matter what holes the balls landed in, the total, on the chart, was blank. The only way a player could get any points was if the person running the game miscounted the numbers and *gave* them some. "Look at it like this," the owner of his first show had said to him, "these people came here to lose. They don't want to win, they want to be entertained. You're in show business, son. You're an entertainer and it's all part of the game."

Red had agreed with him.

"Besides," the owner added, "You're giving them more points, not less. That's what they all want—more points."

Red drank a lot that year. He was making money, but never seemed to be able to hold on to it. He would lose it in poker games. Twice, money was taken from him by force—he was too drunk to resist. Once, in Columbus, Georgia, he didn't even know he was robbed until he woke up the next morning in jail. The owner of the show came and bailed him out.

Red and Tommie graduated to Skillo, the most dangerous of the gambling joints. It attracted the highest stakes and the most aggressive customers.

"That's crazy," Red said, when he first learned what he would have to do to win, "what am I gonna do if someone pulls a gun on me?"

"Play him for the gun," the owner laughed.

It took both of them to run the game properly. Red would stay behind the counter and call in the customers. Tommie stayed out on the midway and mingled with the crowd. Sometimes, he would act like a player to get the action going.

On the counter was a round base much like a small table top. Its outer circumference was lined with small nails spaced about an inch apart. Suspended on a post above the surface of the base was an iron arrow. On the end of that was attached a piece of stiff paper. Between the nails, were written different instructions. Some said: "take out two," or "take out three," or "take out four."

Other spaces were marked to "add" either two, three, or four. The instructions referred to the red wedges which fit in between the nails. A half dozen were in their places between the nails, the others were in a topless cigar box on the counter.

Tommie whistled and pointed out a guy in a knee-length, black leather coat. Most of the people out tonight had jackets or sweaters on, but it was unusual to see someone in an leather coat in Cherokee Point, North Carolina, even in December. Tommie made a sign with his hands telling Red the man had flashed a big roll.

"Right here!" Red yelled at the guy. "Right here! Take a spin—make a win. The only game on the Midway you can beat for cash!"

The guy paused and Red reached out and gave the iron pointer a spin. It went around and around, finally stopping in a spot that said "add two."

The man in the leather coat waited for a young couple to pass, and then crossed the midway. "What's the deal?" he asked.

"Minimum bet is a dollar. You spin the arrow and if you hit a *red*, you win ten to one."

"Here's a dollar," the man said. He put two fingers on the back of the arrow and gave it a gentle push. It went round and round. When it landed in a space marked "add four," the man jumped back in surprise. "Good Lord," he said, "I'm a hot one tonight."

Red took four wedges from the cigar box and added them to the circle. The man in the leather coat put another dollar on the counter and spun again. Red, who could control the movement of the arrow, put him in another space that said "add four." The man whooped with delight. Three or four people passing by, stopped to watch. One of them was Tommie.

"You sure are lucky," Red said, in a submissive tone, as he added wedges.

The man got bolder. "I'll play for two dollars," he said. He spun. This time Red let him win.

The mark was excited. He took a silver flask out of the inside pocket of his coat and took a slug. "Anybody want a drink?" he said to the people watching. He offered it to Red, who declined. Several other people stopped to see what was going on.

"You want to play or not?" Red said angrily.

The man laid the open flask and three dollar bills on the counter. He took three spins in a row—each time adding *reds*. After the third spin, the wheel appeared to be all red. "Go for the jackpot!" someone yelled from the now quite sizable crowd.

"What's the jackpot?" he asked Red.

"You put up two-hundred bucks. If you hit a *red*, you win two-thousand."

"*Two-thousand dollars*," the man said in disbelief.

"He don't even have to spin!" a loud voice from the crowd objected. "It's *all* red!" It was Tommie's voice.

"If he ain't got the money, he can't win!" Red said.

The mark pulled out his wallet. "I got the two-hundred here. You just hold on a second now!" He counted out two-hundred and laid it on the counter.

"Spin it."

The arrow went around and around. It landed in a tiny white space at the back of the circle. "What the fuck?" the man said.

The space was smaller than the others. Red bent over as if to read the writing there. "Says here to take out four."

"Take out four?" The man in the leather coat stretched to read the space. In his haste, he knocked the silver flask to the ground.

Red removed four *reds* from the board. "That's some bad luck there," he said, "better luck next time."

The mark took a slow step backward. His face had paled and all traces of emotion had drained away. "Give me back my money—you little motherfucker."

"I can't give you that money back."

The man kicked the counter with a great surge of energy. "Give me my fuckin' money!"

Tommie saw the gun before Red did. He hit the man in the shoulder with both hands and knocked him to the ground. The gun came loose from the man's grasp and landed next to the silver flask, still spilling whiskey from its open top. Tommie kicked him in the head and ran between two booths toward the back of the midway. Red could not see the man on the ground, because of the counter, but he could see the gun. He pushed the cigar box of wedges where he thought the man was and ran after Tommie.

Later that night, when they were playing cards with a couple of other carnies in their room, they got the news. A man had attacked another redheaded boy who ran a game at the other end of the midway and had cut his throat.

Red *knew* it was the man in the black leather coat who had come back looking for him. Tommie agreed and they left that night for a show in Atlanta.

There, they continued to run Skillo. Red did not see anything wrong in what they were doing, but he feared being caught and he feared losing the respect of the other carnies if he quit. "The hell with 'em," one of them said about the *customers*. "Don't even think about 'em. There ain't a single one of them who would hesitate for a minute to take the money from you, if they could." Red would nod his head and agree. Later, he would drink.

One of the people he would drink with was a carny from Atlanta who ran one of the straight joints. When drunk, Red would brag about how great he "used to" shoot pool and about all the money he had won in Fulton. Finally, after one particularly inflated story, the carny called his bluff.

"You can't play worth shit," he said.

"Yeah, who's gonna beat me," Red replied.

"My friend can."

"Yeah, well, where is he?"

"He's right here—in Atlanta—a place downtown."

Red went with him a few nights later and met his friend. He was tall, dark, and good-looking, about the same age as Red. He introduced himself as "Handsome Danny Jones" and was, as Red discovered, a very strong player. He whistled as he walked around the table, smiling at the two pretty girls waiting for him to finish. Red tried his best, but lost. He returned the next day, the day after that, and the day after that. By the fifth day, he had pulled almost even and didn't stop when it was time to meet Tommie at the show. Late that night, he tied the score and held it there for several hours.

"You're good," Danny said, when they were sitting at the bar later. "You played me to a standstill."

"Man, I was supposed to be running a joint with a friend of mine last night," Red said, "he's gonna be pissed off, but it was worth it."

"You're crazy to be wasting your time in a carnival," Danny said. "You could go anywhere with that pool game and make a living."

Red looked at him. This was one of the *better* players that Oakland Don had spoken about. "You really think so?"

"Hell, yeah, we could go together."

8

CORNBREAD

Detroit Recreation—the largest and finest billiard establishment in the country. Red was amazed. There were three floors of pool, snooker, and billiard tables. There were pretty girls in short skirts who escorted players to their tables and came back at the call of a buzzer when the balls needed racking.

In the elevator coming down from the third floor, Red thought about the past week. He had left Danny Jones in Nashville, after two years on the road together, to go to a famed action room in Cleveland with another player. There, he met yet another guy who bragged about the Detroit scene. The man had not exaggerated. There were poolrooms everywhere—fueled by the bustling auto plants and their resultant prosperity. The immense flow of regular paychecks brought hustlers in from everywhere. Unfortunately, one of them had just cleaned him out.

Stepping from the elevator, he found a pay phone and dug through his wallet for the number. He dialed. When the storekeeper answered, Red asked him to run next door and fetch Thomas. It was the first time he had called since the family moved to Michigan two years ago.

"Is that you, Billy Joe?" Thomas asked when he got on the phone.

"It's me. How are ya doing, Thomas?"

"Glad to hear from you. We were told you died in a big fire down in Atlanta."

"Not me. I'm busted, but I'm definitely not dead."

Thomas came and brought him back to Walled Lake—a forty minute ride from downtown. The family was renting a house there about a block off the lake. Maurine was overjoyed to see him and fixed fried chicken, cabbage, and biscuits—Red's first home cooked meal in months.

"Where are you going to from here, son?" she asked.

"I don't know yet, Ma."

"Why don't you stay here? In Detroit?"

He thought about it. He sure would like to get his money back from that guy at Detroit Recreation.

"Here," Maurine said, handing him a drumstick, "have another piece of chicken."

The big action room in Detroit was the "Hole." It was in the Cass Corridor, just outside the downtown area on Woodward Avenue between Peterborough and Charlotte. It was two doors down from the Motor City Gym, where the best boxers in town trained. The "Majestic Poolroom" was across the street, and a half dozen other rooms were within walking distance.

The first time Red went to the Hole, he was feeling cocky and confident and jumped down the flight of stairs from the sidewalk two steps at a time. Yanking open the door, he stopped at the counter to watch two old guys in an adjoining room argue over a Russian Rummy hand—

neither of them making any sense. When one of them got up and closed the door, Red turned and surveyed the rest of the poolroom. There were sixteen pool tables, two billiard tables, and one six-foot by twelve-foot snooker table.

The best players in town hung out there. "Cowboy" Jimmy Moore was there a lot. So was "Babyface" Al, "Detroit Whitey," Eddie Taylor, and others. These were the *big dogs* that Oakland Don had talked about. Red, who had gotten used to thinking of himself as a top shooter, could not get around these guys. They beat on him unmercifully.

He would go to the neighborhood rooms and take his vengeance out on the locals. His favorite was a room on Harper and Van Dyke, by the Packard plant, where he had a couple dozen regulars in 1953 and 1954. He would bust these auto workers and take the winnings back to the Hole. There, he would match up with one of the top players and get busted himself. It was painful and frustrating. He could not understand why he was losing and was unwilling to accept it. He was like a caged animal—angry and powerless.

One day, in December, he was standing at the bar in a little dive on Third Street, when someone tapped him on the shoulder. He turned around to see a short, curly-headed guy in a white shirt. He was about Red's age, with large ears and a sad expression.

"What do you want?" Red asked.

"I'm here to beat you," the man said.

Red looked him over. "Who the hell are you?"

"I'm Harry Sexton. I play Nine-Ball."

Red had heard of him. He was called the "Bulldog" by some, and "Nine-Ball Harry" by others. Up in Flint, where he came from, people called him "Poochie."

"You the one they call "moochie?" Red asked.

The man ignored his insult. He pointed at the seven-foot bar table in the middle of the room. "I'll play you right here," he said, "five bucks a game."

Red had about thirty dollars in his pocket. He agreed and they flipped for the break.

In less than an hour, Red was down twenty-five bucks and was cussing and slamming the balls around as he racked them. Poochie was at the bar, getting yet another double whiskey. Red could see the end coming, he'd be busted in one or two games. If he had a bigger bank, he could either outbet or outlast this guy. He could stall until the guy was drunk and then kick his ass.

"That's it," he said when Poochie returned. He scattered the balls with his hand and threw the rack down. "I ain't playing any more on this toy table."

"I'll play you on the big tables," Poochie said. "No problem. Come on up to Halligan's in Flint. I'm in there every day."

It was snowing when Red made it up there a couple weeks later. They played Nine-Ball for five on the five and five on the nine. Poochie busted him. Red got hot and started throwing pool balls and breaking sticks. The owner, a big man, physically restrained him, dragged him to the front door, and threw him out. Red stood in front of the plate glass window—yelling and screaming—oblivious to the sub-zero cold.

A couple of months later, he called Halligan's and asked for a rematch.

"I don't think the owner's gonna let you in here," Poochie said.

"I won't get hot again, Harry. Talk to him for me."

The owner agreed to give Red another chance. They played ten on the five and ten on the nine, but still, Red couldn't beat him. He tried to raise the stakes, and got angry when Poochie said no. When he started throwing things, the owner tossed him out again.

Frustrated, he went on the road with Eddie Taylor, the great "Knoxville Bear." They cut a two week swath through the poolrooms of Chicago—drinking and gambling. They would practice during the day and hunt down matches at night. Red watched and learned. He learned about banking, multiple ball shots, and other One-Pocket concepts.

One night they went to a rough honky-tonk on the south side called the "Frontier Club." It was the reputed center of high stakes pool in Chicago. There, Red watched a short, stocky guy in a leather jacket and expensive shoes negotiate a game. He was doing the talking for another player and a small group of backers. He was holding one bottle of beer in his hand and another pressed up against his chest. He was weaving back and forth, waving a thick shank of hundred-dollar bills with his free hand, and slurring his words in a thick Kentucky drawl. Red moved in close, attracted by the money and demeanor. He meant to bet with the man, but when he got close enough to speak—stopped himself. There was something out of kilter, something wrong. He looked until he found it—it was in the man's brown eyes. When perceived together with his voice and mannerisms, they appeared glassy, lost in a vacant, wandering stare. When seen alone, however, there was an intelligence present. The man was calculating at a furious rate, making plans, devising strategy—looking for the chink in someone's armor. Red was impressed and hooked up with him a few days later, when Eddie returned to Detroit. They went on the road together—Red doing the shooting—Beryl handling the money. They went to Ohio, Pennsylvania, and down toward Tennessee. In a small poolroom in West Virginia, they ran into C.P. Bruce.

Red didn't recognize him at first. He looked thinner and older, and was wearing a clerical collar.

"What the hell you doing in that get-up?" Red asked.

"I've found the Lord, Billy Joe. I'm a pastor now."

Red looked to see if he was being spoofed. C.P. was never what you would call an evil man, but he wasn't exactly a saint either. C.P. returned his stare with unflinching eyes. "It's true, Billy Joe."

Red felt awkward and didn't know what to say.

"I'm glad to see you, Billy Joe. I'm glad to see you doing well. You know—" C.P. looked at the floor, then back at Red "—there's a few things I taught you, a few things I showed you—I wish I wouldn't have."

"You were good to me," Red said.

"That's not what I mean. I taught you what I thought was the way to get ahead, the way to survive. Most of what I taught you, I still believe. But I was wrong in some respects."

"What are you talking about, Bruce?"

"Stay honest, Billy Joe. A man can't make it in this life by twisting things around or hiding the truth."

The conversation continued for a few minutes, both of them feeling uncomfortable. When Beryl called from across the room, Red took the opportunity to excuse himself. When he looked around a little later, C.P. Bruce was gone.

By 1957, Red's game had improved a lot. Only Poochie, now the top shooter at the Hole, and maybe a dozen other Detroiters could consistently beat him. When he lost to lesser players, it was from making lopsided games. This overconfidence cost him time and time again, but it was so easy to go out and make a new bankroll, he never learned the lesson. Frustration had turned to a slow burning acceptance of the way things were.

One day in June, he got in a Nine-Ball *ring* game with Poochie, Babyface, Lefty Carbarn, and two other top players. This was a game where each guy, in turn, got his chance to shoot until he missed. When one of them sank the nine-ball, that player won, and everybody else had to pay him. It went on for hours. One player would drop out and somebody new would take his place. All the top players were in it at one point or another. Red, himself, was in it at three different times. He would lose, go and get some more money, get back in, lose again, and go get *more* money to get back in again. He wanted badly to win, but could not pull it off. In the end, Poochie had all the money.

That was the last straw. That was it. He swore he'd do whatever it took to beat these guys. He'd practice, he'd study, he'd stop drinking—whatever it took.

He put himself on a grueling practice schedule. He'd get down to the Hole in the early afternoon and spend three or four hours setting shots up. He'd make a shot and set it up again, then make it and set it up again. He did this over and over until he knew the limitations of that shot and understood the percentage of making it. Sometimes it seemed the more he set a shot up, the more he missed it. It was frustrating as all hell, but he persisted. One day, when he arrived at the Hole, he found two IRS guys putting a lock on the door. They had a sign up that said: 'Closed by order of the U.S. Government.' Red considered this an omen and canned his program.

After that, he practiced by getting into games that were challenging, but not threatening. If he played for only three or four bucks a rack, he could play for hours and not only maintain his sharpness, but increase it. If, during the match, he was confronted with a shot he didn't know or if he made an unexpected mistake, he'd make a mental note of it. Either after the match or the next day, he would shoot that shot until he made it his own.

Fat Art was one of the people he practiced with. He wasn't as challenging as Red would have liked, but he was entertaining and likable. He was a fat guy. Not a soft and dumpy fat guy, but a waddling and big-in-the-butt fat guy. No one could tell exactly *how fat* because of the immense pants he wore. They were two or three sizes larger than his blue rayon shirt and had the deepest pockets anyone in the pool hall had ever seen. They disappeared into the vast, black pleats of those shiny trousers and revealed no hint whatsoever of the contents thereof.

To play with Fat Art was like being at a magic show. One never knew what to expect. Once, Red was walking around the table to get to a shot when he saw Art's hand disappear into a pocket, pause, and come back out with a banana!

Red broke out laughing, as did the small group of people watching them practice.

In the next game, Red was at the table chalking his stick, when he looked at Fat Art, now eating a peanut butter sandwich. Red, realizing it had probably been in one of those huge pockets for hours, cracked up again.

Red played every chance he got. He took Oakland Don's advice to heart and doggedly pursued every top player in town and every road player who came to town. People began to talk about him, to seek him out for the action he could deliver. Many times he was beaten, and forced to regroup, but little by little he was advancing. The first top honcho fell to him in a handicapped match with Red getting the spot. Shortly after, he beat the same man even up. A few weeks later, another top dog was toppled. Every time he played one of these players, he made it a point to learn something. He learned to recognize the proper shots and moves. He began to understand how he had beaten himself in the past and he learned to project confidence and dominance. Most importantly, he learned, a little at a time, to control his anger.

The more confident he became, the better he played. The better he played, the more confident he became. He started to think of himself as having a destiny—that he was a winner—that the game of pool belonged to him.

He began to move around the table with a faster pace, a greater sureness, a simplicity of movement. His stroke developed a natural smoothness and rhythm. Without consciously trying, he picked up what was called a *slipstroke*. During his practice strokes he held the cue stick forward of where it would normally be held. In the final backstroke, he let it slip into its proper place a split second before delivering the stroke to the cue ball. It was a thing of beauty.

Confidence opened the floodgates of personality. He became quick to speak, usually not knowing what he was saying until he said it. As the number of players who could beat him became smaller and smaller, he began to feel invincible—indestructible. When he was beaten, this feeling would subside for a day or two, then return at an even higher intensity. In his mind, he was back in Fulton—walking down Main Street with his shirt unbuttoned to the waist.

He became a favorite of the bookies and the high-stake gamblers. They liked his style and they liked being associated with him. Red found it easy to stake a game, something that made him attractive to other players. Everybody wanted to play him. He became an individual, a distinct character in the sea of pool players.

Most of the top players Red knew, or had heard of, had nicknames. It came with being recognized and was considered a badge of respect—a mark of acceptance. Some were named after physical characteristics like "One-eye Pete" or "Babyface." Others were named after their origins like "Cuban Joe" and "Oakland Don"—others, for their style: "Bulldog," for his tenacity, "Machinegun Lou," for his fast pace. If Red had a nickname, he could introduce himself as "they call me so-and-so." He had tried it with "The Paducah Kid," but it never caught on. He wondered if he would ever be known by any name besides Red or Billy Burge.

One day, on the way back from Walled Lake, he stopped at a small poolroom in downtown Pontiac. He was sitting at a table eating the cornbread and chicken Maurine had insisted he take with him. About twenty feet away, a bookie and a car salesman were arguing at the counter.

"Nobody, but nobody, can beat my boy playing one-handed," the bookie said, indicating a Puerto Rican practicing on one of the tables.

"So what?" the other said, "who plays one-handed?"

"Give us the eight and the break, and your boy can play two-handed."

"Bullshit."

"You say bullshit? I'll bet you a thousand dollars."

"What if I get *him*?" he pointed at Red.

"I don't care who you get."

"Hey, Red!" The salesman yelled. "Come on over here."

Red picked up the rest of his meal and walked to the counter. "What's up?" he asked.

"You want to play his boy for a thousand?" he pointed to the man practicing.

Red looked at the short, dark man pocketing balls with his cue stick delicately balanced in one hand. He was dressed fastidiously, with a little green apron around his waist to keep the table dirt off his trousers. Red turned his head to look at the bookie. When their eyes met, the bookie asked, "What's in the paper?"

"Just a little cornbread," Red replied.

They worked out the details of the match and began to play. The bookie, in an attempt to distract him, kept referring to him as "cornbread." In the beginning, it was said with a derogatory tone of voice. Later, as Red tore "his boy" up, it took on a hint of respect. By the time the match was over, he was calling him "Cornbread Red" and telling everyone how he was going to take him to Chicago. "We'd make a killing there," he said.

In a matter of days, the story of the game and the name, had gotten around town. Everywhere he went they were calling him "Cornbread Red." A few days later, Billy Burge was but a memory—Cornbread Red had arrived.

9

RULES OF THE ROAD

Cornbread Red made the rounds of the poolrooms and action bars on a regular basis. He had bird dogs in most places who would call him if a well-loaded stranger or a hot-to-trot road hustler wandered in. The first thing he would do each day, after showering, was call a half dozen rooms to see who was in—what was happening. Often, he'd place a wager on a game in progress without even being there. He was on the constant lookout for action. Cornbread Red, like other gamblers, loved the high. He loved having it all riding on one game—on one shot. It was like a drug. He couldn't get enough of the rush, the excitement, the suspense.

He was checking out a room on the lower east side where he knew two of the hustlers. Both were what was referred to as *locksmiths*. They were only average players, but excellent gamblers. They didn't get many games, but they never lost the ones they did. They never played unless it was a lock—with no possibility of the other guy winning. Some players held this in contempt, but few were above getting a side bet down when someone *had the nuts*.

Red walked in the front door and ten feet into the poolroom. He stopped and looked around. "There's no goddamn pool players in here," he yelled, loud enough for everyone to hear. "There ain't a single motherfucker in here who would bet ten cents that water's wet!"

"Hey, man—don't be talking that shit in here. There's a lot of good players in here, and you know it," the man at the counter said.

"Players?" Red said, making a face. "Ain't nobody in here but *alligators*."

"Alligators?"

"That's right. A bunch of alligators sitting in the water with their mouths open—letting the flies in. They won't tangle with something that'll fight back. They're just waiting for enough flies to make a mouthful."

"Hey, Cornbread!" came a voice from the back of the room. It was Fat Art, in what appeared to be the same blue rayon shirt, playing one of the locksmiths. Red walked back, nodded at the hustler, and shook hands with Art.

"You going to the Hustler's Convention, Cornbread?" Art asked.

"What are you talking about?"

"Johnston City, the World's All-Around Hustler's Championship. All the best players in the world are gonna be there."

Red looked at the hustler, who confirmed it. "That's right," he said, "they started it last year. Fats was there. So was Squirrel and Daddy Warbucks. It goes on for almost a month."

"You should be going, Cornbread," Art said. "They're gonna have the world's tournament for Nine-Ball, one for Straight Pool, one for One-Pocket, and one for the all-around championship. You're good enough, you should be there."

"You'd be crazy to go," said the hustler. "You won't win, and when it's over, every player in the worlds gonna know who you are and how you play. You won't get another game for the rest of your life."

Red thought about it on his way back to Highland Park. The hustler was probably right, but the idea of spending a month gambling, drinking, and shooting pool with the top players in the world was too big of an attraction to pass up. He threw a few items in the car and left that evening.

The car broke down in western Michigan, and he spent a big hunk of his bankroll on repairs. When it broke again in Indiana, he abandoned it and hitchhiked. He was picked up by another hustler going to the tournament. They drove through Indiana and into the flatlands of southern Illinois, the Little Egypt section, where Red had been with Oakland Don almost fifteen years before. They passed the federal prison at Marion and continued south to Johnston City. It was dark when the driver dropped Red off in the parking lot of the Jansco Showbar.

There was a sign by the front door welcoming the public to "the finest and largest night club in the Midwest, and The World's Hustler's Championship, your hosts: George and Paul Jansco." He walked into a restaurant complete with candles and white tablecloths. He recognized none of the twenty or so diners, most of whom were working on thick steaks. He walked through the restaurant and into a nightclub complete with dance floor and bar. He asked the bartender for the "tournament room," and was directed to "the pit." When he got there, he was surprised. It was a sunken room surrounded on three sides by bleachers. The far wall was lined with a long flat table, with several trophies on it. Above, a huge elimination chart was taped to the wall. In the middle of the room were two immaculate pool tables with brilliant, new cloth. The only person in the room was leveling one.

"Where is everybody?" Red asked.

"All the action's back behind the Showbar," the guy said and pointed.

Red walked out the back door. Across a parking lot of Cadillacs and Buicks, was a square, block building. A sign above that door read: "Cue Club of America— members only." He pulled the door open and went inside. Here was the scene he was looking for. There were two rooms, five pool tables, and a bar along one wall. Smoke hung to the ceiling like loose fog. Men were standing in small groups, some speaking in hushed, furtive voices— others loud and boisterous.

Red recognized several players. Kilroy from "Market Billiards" in Detroit was there. They had passed a few good games on to each other over the years. The "Jockey" from Detroit was there. So was Jimmy Moore. The tall, slender guy with the receding hairline and the fine clothes was Bill "Weenie Beanie" Staton. Red had seen him on TV. At the end of the bar was New York Fats, already calling himself after one of the characters in the movie, "The Hustler," released a few months before.

Red stepped to the crowded bar and ordered a beer. He leaned back on one elbow, and surveyed the scene. A tall, craggy faced man, a top player Red knew as "Toledo," was playing One-Pocket with a chunky fellow on the closest table. Several people were watching and talking about the game. A couple of them had money in their hands. Red cocked an ear to try and overhear what they were playing for.

"Hey, look what the cat dragged in," a loud voice said in his other ear. He turned to see a dark, handsome, familiar face.

"Danny!" He jumped back in surprised delight, the great smile on his face matched by the one on "Handsome" Danny Jones.

They ordered a bottle of champagne and joked and jived their way through the first glass. Red poured each of them another. "What's going on here?" he asked, nodding toward the One-Pocket game.

"They're playing for three-hundred a game. I've got fifty on Toledo."

"Who's the other guy?"

"His name is Albert DeFozio. I don't know much about him, but he don't play too good. Toledo's giving him eight to six and kicking his butt."

They watched the game and drank the champagne. When Albert DeFozio finally quit, both Red and Danny had bets down against him. They got another bottle of champagne to celebrate and finished off the night with it.

◆   ◆   ◆

Kilroy was a man of average height, with a barrel chest, and powerful arms. He was a likable man who looked tough, knew it, and did his best to live up to it. Often unshaved, he smoked Pall Malls one after another, sometimes down to the very end. He would hold the burning butt in his lips until the person he was talking with was forced to cry out: "Hey! You're gonna burn your lip." He liked it when they tried to brush away the tiny butt with their hand, like he didn't know what he was doing. He understood pool and gambling—and he understood control.

He was at the bar in the Cue Club with Johnny Irish, a thin, pale man, one of the best players in the world. They watched as Cornbread Red came through the door, back from playing his first tournament match in the pit. "I know him from Detroit," Kilroy said, "he was watching Toledo and Albert lay down the *spread* for about five hours last night."

"I know who he is, too," Irish said. "I played him down south a couple of years ago. He's a sucker. He doesn't know how good he is and he doesn't know how good a *good* player is. If he's got any money, it's a cinch to take it. If you miss once, he'll give you the eight-ball. If you miss again, he'll give you the seven."

They watched as Albert DeFozio took the place next to Cornbread at the bar, ordered a drink from the bartender, and paid for it with a bill peeled from a large roll.

Albert and Toledo were friends. They had arrived in Johnston City separately to keep that fact concealed. Last night they had played One-Pocket for three-hundred dollars a game. Every dime of the money exchanged back and forth was Albert's. He had deliberately played below his real skill level and Toledo, who had spotted him two balls, appeared to have beat him badly. The dozen or so people who knew the scoop, now watched as Albert and Red set up a game. No one spoke to Red or tried to warn him. It was part of the hustler's code—*don't mess with another man's game.* A player was considered solely responsible for the games he made.

Red agreed to play the best of ten games of One-Pocket for five-hundred. He only had about three-fifty, but he expected to win. If he got caught *playing on nerve*, if he lost and was unable to pay, he planned to get it from Danny.

Based on Albert's previous performance, Red spotted him ten to eight. He would have to pocket ten balls in his pocket before Albert got eight in his. Most people in the know would have bet on Albert if the handicap was reversed. As it was, there was very little betting, everyone wanted DeFozio, no one wanted Red.

The action was on the other tables. Don Willis had a proposition shot going and was cleaning up. Fats was beating a college kid to death and razzing him without mercy all the while. On another table, Eddie Taylor and another man were in a fiercely contested game of Banks—where all shots had to be bank shots. There was even more commotion coming from the general direction of the adjoining card room. The only eyes on the game between DeFozio and Cornbread, were the ones who wanted to see how this young redhead would handle getting his leg caught in a *trap*.

It was in the sixth game that Red realized his predicament. Albert made a move that revealed a whole concept of One-Pocket that he had appeared ignorant of last night. Red noticed Kilroy at one of the tables and walked over and bummed a cigarette.

"Are they booking my match?" he asked, referring to the group of bookies at the bar.

"Nobody wanted you, Red."

Red took a long drag on the Pall Mall and blew it out slowly as he nodded his head. "Great," he said, "I'm in a trap—ain't I?"

Kilroy nodded slightly, his head barely moving.

Red thought of asking Kilroy to get Danny for him, but didn't. He walked back to the bar and his glass of Crown Royal. It was half-full. He threw it down in one swallow, and as the warmth hit and began to spread, he felt a fire of another sort. It, too, started in the pit of his stomach. God, how he hated being hemmed in. How he hated being controlled—just like that *motherfucker Charlie* and the *goddamn jail*. He slapped the glass upside-down on the bar, stabbed the cigarette in the ash tray, and walked to the table and picked up his cue stick.

He played like a man possessed, not saying a word or in any way acknowledging the presence of anyone or anything else in the room. He was in a world of his own, cold and focused. He was the raw realization of intention—nothing distracted him.

At one point, when he became aware of having just run eight and out, he heard someone quietly call his name. It was Kilroy, a glass of whiskey in his outstretched hand. "Here," he said, "it's Crown Royal."

Red took the drink, still not speaking.

"I put a hundred on you," Kilroy whispered.

Red turned his attention back to the table, a new rack of balls now sitting there waiting for him. He broke, the cue ball rolling gently to the far rail and spinning to the side rail and back up behind the pack. Four balls moved toward his pocket, none toward Albert's. One ball teetered on the edge of Red's pocket for what seemed like a full second, and then fell in. An absolutely perfect One-Pocket break.

By the end of the match, Red had gone from intense and under pressure to cocksure and arrogant. He was sure of the win, awash in the whiskey that kept coming—blustering, loud, and brash. "Play with me, and I'll send you to the pawn shop," he shouted, to no one in particular. "I'll put you on welfare! I'll beat you so bad, you'll need a brain surgeon!" He was shooting fast and loose, without aiming; without thinking.

He won and Albert declined to play anymore. Red stayed at the bar and tried to drink everything that was bought for him. Kilroy helped.

"He deserves everything he gets," Kilroy said late that night. They were half-drunk—talking about the movie "The Hustler," and how Fats had capitalized on it.

"They put him down, but they all try and imitate him."

"Nobody can imitate Fatty. No one can talk that talk, no one can walk that walk. They used to call him Triple-Smart Fats, you know."

"He's smart enough to have half the world thinking he can shoot pool," Red said, taking a swallow.

"Hey, don't make a mistake about that, Red. He *can* shoot pool."

"Yeah, well I met a hundred guys on the road that can shoot better than he can."

"What? You some kind of authority on road players?" Kilroy asked.

"I been on the road all my life," Red replied, "I was on the road before they even had roads."

"You're no road player," Kilroy said, "You're a forty-miler. You been to Bay City and Lansing—places like that. You got no serious time under your belt."

"I been all around the world. Played more millionaires than even the fat man has."

"Cornbread, you don't even know the rules of the road."

"Rules of the road?" Red said, "what rules?"

Kilroy looked up at the ceiling in disbelief. "I can't believe you don't know the rules of the road. Hey, Irish," he yelled across the room, "come on over here and tell Cornbread Red the rules of the road."

Johnny Irish came and joined them at the bar. "That was a hell of a shoot-out you had, Red. You've brought your game up a couple of notches since we played."

"Thanks," Red said, "what about these rules I'm supposed to know?"

"Man, you ain't supposed to come to a Hustler's Convention and not know the rules."

"Just fucking tell me, all right?"

"Okay, okay, don't lose your temper. The first rule a hustler has to know before he goes on the road is—" he paused— "always carry a heavy blanket."

Kilroy laughed. It took a second for Red, who was expecting something serious, to realize he was being spoofed. He laughed too.

"Number two is: You have to develop an appetite for canned foods—such as pork and beans."

Two other guys drifted over to the conversation. One of them was laughing already. "What's number three, Irish?" the guy asked.

"When you check into a hotel, make sure you always get a first floor room."

"Tell 'em why, Irish," Kilroy said.

"So your suitcase doesn't break when they throw it out."

All of them were laughing now.

"Also," Irish continued, "it helps to know where the six dollar rooms are."

"And you have to learn how to sleep comfortably in a car," Kilroy added.

Red tried one of his own. "If you get tired, take one of those little yellow jobs."

Everyone laughed except Irish. "Taking pills is a bunch of bullshit," he said. "You take a pill, he takes a pill. You take another, so does he. What's the point? If you're tired, go get some sleep. The worst that can happen is you'll get the same game tomorrow as you're getting today."

The small group of men responded with halfhearted grunts of agreement. They knew it was true, but all of them had a pill or two in their pocket—just to make sure.

Kilroy broke the silence. "Hey, don't forget the most important rule of all."

"That's right," Irish said. "The most important rule of all—for all hustlers—is—" he paused for effect. "Don't forget to win."

Everybody agreed with enthusiasm.

10

GAMBLERS AND CHAMPIONS

That first year at Johnston City opened up the whole thing for Red. Like a gunfighter of the old west, who had reached his prime and earned his reputation, Red had arrived. He had found his place and bought his freedom. But, like the gunfighter, it was a trap. It was too late to turn back, too late to change course, and too easy to continue. He became a member of a loose fraternity of the hundred-or-so top pool players in the country. One of them, Earl Shrieber, helped him make a profitable entrance. He backed Red against the hustlers who hadn't met him yet. "Act like you don't play so good," he said. Red did—and they cleaned up. Earl taught him some of the finer points of making games. He taught him how to evaluate an opponent and how to handicap intelligently. "People always ask for something, but they don't hardly ever ask for enough," he said. "When you're doing the asking, make sure you ask for enough."

When he wasn't in a game, Red would hang out at the bar and listen to the hustling stories. Some of them were unbelievable.

"Look at Bunny over there shooting one-handed," Kilroy said, one night. "You wouldn't believe some of the things he's done. He shoulda been in the movies. We used to call him "Keep-The-Motor-Running"—he got chased out of so many joints."

"He's crazy as a loon," Red said.

"He's crazy like a fox. I was on the road with that little guy for almost a year."

"What happened?" Danny asked.

Kilroy lit a Pall Mall and blew out the match. "I would drop him off at a bar. He'd go in there with this checkered sport coat on—carrying a cigar box with holes punched in the lid, with a great big fat rubber band around it."

Red and Danny laughed at the image.

"He'd go up to the bar, put that cigar box on the bar, and order a beer—all the time doing that 'St. Vitus Dance' bit of his. 'A shell of beer, please,' he'd say real shaky-like. Then he'd pull out his wallet to pay and drop the thing on the floor. Money falls all over from it—he drops about half of it trying to pick it up and put it back in the wallet. A real loser. All of this in front of two mooches playing Eight-Ball for five dollars." Kilroy flicked the ashes in the ash tray as another guy joined the conversation. "He gets his beer and his change. He takes a quarter to the table and puts it real gently on the rail. 'I challenge' he says in that squeaky voice. The mooches—they go 'hey buster, we're playing for money here—take a seat'—you know, real big timers. 'I know my rights,' Bunny whines. Finally, they don't want to take advantage of him or anything, but they remember all that *money*!"

All of them are laughing now. Red orders a round from the bar girl.

"They're just about ready to let him play. Bunny calls the bar girl over and says 'Where's the mmmen's rooom?' Just like that. She points and he says 'Watch my bbbox please. Don't let anyone touch it.' He starts to walk away and turns around real quick. 'Don't look in my bbbbox.' he says to her. The mooches are rolling their eyes. They can't believe this."

"Well, you know she's gonna look in there," Danny says.

"All *three* of them look in there!" Kilroy exclaims. "They pull that rubber band off and open that lid. They can't believe what's in there."

He pauses until Red asks, "What's in there?"

"A fuckin' toad!"

They all laughed. Danny, who was swallowing at the punch line, choked as whiskey went down the wrong pipe. Red slapped him on the back.

When everyone settled down, Kilroy continued with the story. "When he comes back, these guys are ready to play. They got a *live one*. Bunny goes 'I don't play for no chicken feeds.' Sure enough, they go for it."

"And you're outside with the motor running, right?" Danny ventured.

"No way. I'm walking by the front window about every five minutes. Bunny's giving me the hand signals— letting me know how it's going. When he's got the money and they're beginning to get on to him, he gives me the hot sign. I come busting in the door. 'Bernard!' I say. 'There you are. I've been looking all over town for you. Your poor mother is worried sick about you.' I act like I just then notice the two mooches and the pool table. I make a face like this." He makes a face of exasperation. "Oh, Bernard,' I say. 'Have you lost your entire disability check again?' I grab him by the arm and start leading him to the door."

"What do the guys say?" Red asked.

"Sometimes they don't say anything. Most of the time one of them will say something like: 'Hey, wait a minute. He's got our money.' I just blow them off. I say: 'You should be ashamed of yourself. Gambling with an invalid.' We get to the car as fast as we can."

"That's a hell of a story," Red said. The others agreed.

"That ain't nothing. There's lots more," Kilroy said.

◆   ◆   ◆

Over the next few years, the Johnston City Tournament and the Stardust Tournament, started in Vegas by the Jansco's, were the highlights of Red's life. The Stardust was seventeen days in March. Johnston City was almost a month, near the end of October. In 1963, ABC Television, in the form of "The Wide World of Sports," came to the Illinois tournament. Red loved it.

He was known nationally by then, but only in the billiard community. Unlike many of the hustlers who preferred to stay anonymous, Red thrived on exposure. He liked the attention he saw Minnesota Fats receiving and wanted it for himself.

Once, he got to do trick shots on "The Wide World of Sports." Besides that, the closest he came to fame was chasing Fats. "They call you Cornbread Red now," Fats said in his inimitable style, "but they'll be calling you No-bread Red when I'm through with you."

"Yeah, you gonna be a thin man when I get through with you," Red countered. It went back and forth like that. Red won on the table right from the start, but Fats won with the mouth. Red couldn't keep up.

One year, he shared a taxi out of Johnston City with "Titanic" Thompson. Titanic, who got his name by claiming to be a survivor of the ship, was a proposition man. He was famous for always having something outlandish to bet on. Sports Illustrated and Golf Digest had both done stories on him. People were always willing to bet him, and he was always winning. He'd brag he could hit a golf ball a mile and when the doubtful put money up, he'd take them to Pikes Peak or out on a frozen lake and whack it out of sight.

One time he bet a doctor how far his house was from the edge of town. The doctor swore it was less than ten miles. "I drive that way every day to get to my office," he said. "I've driven it a thousand times. It's exactly nine and three-quarters of a mile from my house to the city limits."

"Bet you five-thousand," Titanic said.

"You're on," the doctor said.

They drove out to measure the distance in the doctor's car. They were followed by three carloads of guys eager to find out who won. They measured the distance with the odometers on all four vehicles. All of them registered over ten miles. Back at the showbar, the doctor paid up. "I can't believe I was wrong!" he cried as he forked out the cash.

In the cab, Cornbread asked what happened. "With that doctor?" Titanic replied, "Ahhh, he's always bragging how good he knows the area, grew up here and everything. I sent a guy out there the night before and had him dig up the city limit sign and move it down the road. Hey!" he said to the driver, "take a left here." He turned back to Red, "Thieving cabbies—think we just got off the boat or something."

Red watched as the cab turned.

"That was a good game you played Fats," Titanic said. "What are you gonna do with the money?"

"Play pool. Maybe go to the horse track with Kilroy. He's gonna teach me to play 'em."

"Don't do it."

"What do you mean?"

"You ever see anybody who plays the horses have anything? No. You haven't. If you play the horses, you end up with nothing. Period. Look at your friend Kilroy. He's got nothing. No wife, no life, no nothing, just those horses. But look at the bookies, everyone of them is driving a Cadillac. Stay away from the horses and stay away from Kilroy if he tries to take you there."

"He loves those horses," Red said.

"Everybody loves horses. You ever hear of anyone who didn't love horses?" he paused and looked at Red for an answer. "Stay away from the horses, son, don't be a fool."

"Kilroy tells me that he ran two dollars up to over thirteen-thousand one time. That's no fool business. That's serious business."

"Don't bullshit me, Cornbread, and don't bullshit yourself. You got talent with pool. Stay with it—you've got an element of control there. You've got nothin' with the horses. You don't know what the jockeys are doing, you don't know what the owners are doing, and you don't even know what the horses are doing! I've seen guys lose everything—millions. Win fifty, lose five-hundred—over and over and over again."

Red was quiet.

"Look," Titanic said, "give me your phone number. If I get something cooking, I'll send for you."

"Great," Red said.

Later, he told Danny about it.

"You better be careful," Danny said.

"Careful? I'm ready to tap some of that heavy money, and it doesn't get any heavier than Titanic."

"Yeah, everybody thinks it's great running with him," Danny said. "Live the good life and all that shit."

"He's a great man," Red said.

"Maybe, but he's definitely crazy. When Little Hand was running with him he had to go in the hotel room first, so Titanic could come in behind with a shotgun. He told Little Hand: 'If it's a heist, you drop to the floor—I'll take care of it.' Man, I can't live like that, I'd rather be broke."

Red believed the story. He had heard Titanic was always heeled. Not just one gun, but two. He was a champion shooter and a champion quick draw. As a matter of fact, Red thought, he was also a champion golfer. Too bad he couldn't shoot pool—couldn't make a straight-in shot.

"What's the matter with me?" he was always asking. "Why can't I play this game?" No one knew.

At Johnston City, trophies were handed out for each of four championships. One was for Straight Pool, one was for One-Pocket, and another was for Nine-Ball. The winners of these three championships played off for the fourth trophy—The All-Around Championship of the World—King of the Hill.

Red fared better at the gambling than he did in the tournaments. For him, the question was: 'Why can't I do good in these tournaments?' Red would gamble with players and hold his own, but lose to the same guys in a tournament. He even played partners with Harold Worst, who won the All-Around in 1965, and he *always* held his end of the deal up.

Once, when they were gambling with another pair, Red was surprised to see Harold unscrewing his stick. "What are you doing , Harold? We can beat these guys."

"Never had a doubt about it," Harold replied. "But it's midnight." He pointed to the clock on the wall.

Red was puzzled. "So what?" he said, "who are you, Cinderella?"

"No," Harold laughed, "it's Sunday. I don't play pool on Sunday—it's the Sabbath."

"Are you serious?"

"Absolutely."

After Harold left the room, Red finished up and won, playing both his and Harold's turns.

The next year, back in Johnston City, Red had his best tournament showing. He went through the One-Pocket field like a lion through lambs. No one could stop him. All the way to the finals—Cornbread Red versus Ed Kelly for the 1966 One-Pocket Championship of the World.

Red started the match with strength and determination. Ed Kelly fought back with the same. It was what pool players called a *dogfight*. It came down to the last ball of the last game. Red had a fairly easy shot at his corner. It was a bit of a stretch, but a routine shot nevertheless. A couple of the guys who were betting on Ed Kelly, were already passing money to the victors. "You put up a hell of a fight," Red said as he lined up the shot. Ed Kelly, who was sitting in the player's chair with a dejected look on his face, suddenly brightened. He motioned frantically for the referee's attention. Red, who was facing the opposite way, was not aware of what was going on between them. The referee moved over just in time to see what Ed Kelly was so excited about. Red, stretching for the shot, had both feet off the floor.

"Foul!" the referee yelled.

"Foul? What the hell do you mean—foul?" Red jumped off the table like a man attacked.

"Both feet off the floor," the referee said. "It's your shot," he pointed at Kelly.

Red tried to argue the point. "That's bullshit," he said, "I been playing here for two weeks and no one has ever called a bullshit foul like that on anyone."

"You been playing for two weeks in the back room," the referee said. "You can make up your own rules there, but in here, we play by the tournament rules. Sit down and let Ed shoot." It was an easy out for Kelly, who became the 1966 One-Pocket Champion of the World.

After the match, Red was in the Cue Club. He was drinking, gambling, and bullshitting. With second-place money and honors, he was still in the center of attention and loving every minute of it. He was bantering with one of the bookmakers, trying to get better odds on a game in process, when he looked up to see Jack Grady, the barber, standing there.

"Hey, everybody, look at this," Cornbread yelled. "The first man who ever bet on me. Hey, Jack. How are you?" Red clapped him on the back, almost hugging him.

"I'm good, Billy Joe. I saw on TV you were gonna be here. I drove up from Fulton."

"I just played for the championship a few minutes ago," Red said. "Did you see it?"

"Yessiree, I sure did," Jack said. "You've come a long way, Billy Joe."

"Did you bring C.P. Bruce?"

"He couldn't make it, Billy Joe."

"I can't believe it. Here I'm playing for the Championship of the World in his favorite game, and he won't even drive a hundred miles to see me?"

"He passed away last summer, Billy Joe."

"Man, you're kidding."

"About two weeks after Oakland Don."

"Oh, man—" Red turned away, took a slow breath, and shook his head in disbelief. "I need a drink," he said.

For the next few months both C.P. and Don were on Red's mind. In the past, he thought of them from time to time when a particular shot would jar his memory. He would sometimes *hear* either C.P. or Oakland Don coaching him through it as they had years before. Ever since Jack told him of their deaths, however, he found himself thinking about them all the time—driving in the car—sitting in the john—trying to get to sleep. It pushed him to do something to get his mind off of it. He'd drink, or get in a game—any kind of interaction with someone else—a card game, a crap game, flip a coin—anything.

That year he went to the Stardust Tournament as usual. He got in the money with an average performance, but what he did on the craps table was nothing less than astounding. Starting with twenty-six dollars, Red got hot. He was playing the odds and throwing passes—over and over. It was as if the green felt of the craps table was the green felt of the pool table and answered to his control just like the pool table did when he hit his stride. He'd need to throw an eight—he'd see it in his mind—throw— and get an eight. Once, he threw fourteen sevens and elevens in a row before getting a point.

Many of the tournament players were on the casino floor. When word got around that Red was on a roll, dozens of them congregated around the crap table—

betting the pass line with him, cheering him on. Red was intoxicated with the energy, the excitement, and the exquisite pleasure of a crystal clear state of mind. It was like magic. He was throwing back the drinks passed to him by the casino girls—tucking black, hundred-dollar chips down their cleavage in return.

When he finally crapped out, he had amassed over ninety-five-thousand dollars. Back in the tournament room, he passed hundred-dollar bills out to whoever asked for one. He staked a half dozen games and bought endless drinks. He was celebrating—spending money like it was green stamps—the Cornbread Red way.

In the afternoon, he was drinking with "Junior," "The Meatman," and two other friends. "I'm gonna go to that fancy store in the hotel and get a brand new wardrobe," Red said.

"Hey, take us with you," one of his buddies said.

"Come on."

When they came through the door of the pricey shop, they looked like a rough bunch. They were loud and smelled of alcohol. A concerned clerk met them in the front of the store. "Can I help you gentlemen?"

"Damn right," Red bellowed, "I wanna buy these boys some duds."

The clerk looked like he thought it was a stick-up. "What items did you have in mind, sir?" he asked, struggling to stay composed.

Red lit a cigarette. "It's a quarter to three," he said, pointing at the clock. "Whatever these boys pick out before three o'clock, I'll pay for."

When the clerk hesitated, Red reached into his pocket and pulled out a two-and-a-half-inch roll of bills. He pulled the red rubber band off and thumbed them—all hundreds.

The next fifteen minutes were a frantic swirl of pants, shirts, alligator shoes, and measuring tapes. Red's friends realized about halfway through that sizes did not matter. Sizes could be exchanged tomorrow—the *crucial* element was time. They started pulling things off hangers and throwing them on the counter. When it was over, Red gave the flabbergasted clerk close to fifteen-thousand.

On the way back to the tournament room, they ran into Fats, holding court with a bunch of tourists in the casino. There were two businessmen with him—possibly TV or casino executives.

"Hey, Fats!" Red yelled. "Come on, I'll play you for fifty-thousand right now."

Fats tried to ignore him.

"You afraid of me, Fats? Come on—you get on TV and tell everyone you're the best. Let's put some money on it."

Fats made a crack to his audience that Red couldn't hear. They tittered.

"Come on," Red yelled again. "I got the money in the casino safe. We can play right now. You don't wanna play me, I'll back Kelly against you for twenty-thousand."

Fats left the people he was with and came up close to Red and his friends. "Don't embarrass me in front of these people, Cornbread."

"All right," Red said, "but the next time you get something going, you better call me."

Fats agreed and Red and his friends returned to the tournament room. Red made a deal with one guy to invest in a poolroom down in Tampa. He gave him several thousand and bought a round of drinks to seal the deal. A day and a half later, Red was broke.

11

THE APOLLO

The call from Fats came in June. He had a new TV series being filmed live out of Chicago. It was called "Fats Hustles the Pros." Would Red like to come and be on it? It paid a thousand dollars if he won and seven-fifty if he lost. Red jumped at the chance and they played a couple of weeks later. They played a set of Nine-Ball, a game of One-Pocket, and a game of Straight Pool. Red won all three—a shutout.

On his way back to Detroit, he stopped in Benton Harbor, a small city on the shores of Lake Michigan. It was *the* place to stop on the road from Chicago to Detroit. Having a population of only fifteen-thousand, it boasted six healthy poolrooms. Red had heard from Fats that a hustler by the name of Norman hung out there in a place called the Apollo Bar. "He'll play," Fats had said.

The Apollo was in a long, narrow building. It had a bar running the entire length of the left wall and half a dozen cocktail tables in front. The bathroom and pinball machines were in the back, by the door to the alley. When Red asked at the counter for Norman, the bartender pointed to a large, blond man playing pinball. As Red watched, he tilted the machine and swore in a deep voice. Cornbread walked up and touched him on the sleeve. "I understand you play a little pool," he said, leaving it hanging like a question.

The man looked up, already digging into his pocket for more change. "Cornbread Red—seen you on the tube. You looked good."

"Hell, that wasn't me," Red said, "that was my brother. I can't play half what he does."

Norman laughed and put a quarter in the machine. "You looking for a game Cornbread?"

"Sure."

"I play Nine-Ball. We can play across the street. He'll stay open for us if we want."

Red hesitated. "Man, I don't want to play any of that ninny ball. Fatty wore me out on that fool game. You're a player—lets play One-Pocket. I'll play you on a snooker table for a thousand a game."

"Not gonna happen, Cornbread. This is Nine-Ball town. It's the national pastime here. I can wait until closing time at Bendix and take my pick of fish to play—for more money than you're carrying." He pulled the plunger back and shot a silver ball into the machine. "You came here, Cornbread—if you want to play—it's Nine-Ball."

Red liked that kind of talk. "I'll play you for two-hundred a game," he said.

They left immediately and went across the street to Sarge's Poolroom. The front half of the building was a barber shop. It was the same as Jack Grady's place in Fulton—the same smells of soap and leather. The poolroom was in back—four tables and a respectful degree of privacy. It was the unadvertised place for big action in Benton Harbor.

Red made a mental note to use the barber shop to freshen up later. According to Fats, Norman had a reputation among road players of having great staying power and sometimes lasted thirty or forty hours before he lost, or *went off* as pool players called it. Lots of other times it was the other guy who *went off*. Red understood that style, as it was the same as his own—just wear 'em out. Yes, a shave and a hot towel in about eight hours could make the difference between winning or losing.

Several people had followed them over from the bar—others had evidently gone elsewhere to pass the word. By the time Red stopped in the john, threw some water on his face, and got to the table, there were already twenty-some people seated in anticipation. As he put his stick together, a thin guy came over and introduced himself.

"I'm Don Alabaster," he said, "They call me Al. I own the bar 'cross the street—the Apollo." His mouth barely moved as he spoke, the thin mustache remaining motionless.

Red did not like being interrupted at the beginning of a game. He grunted and reluctantly shook the extended hand.

"You got yourself a tough game here, Cornbread. Would you be interested in spreading the risk around?"

"What do ya want to do?"

"How about I cover half your action?"

Red considered the offer. It was true. This could end up being a tough match for him. "All right," he said, looking Al in the face, "but if I lose, I don't want to hear none of that bullshit."

"What do you mean?"

"If I lose, I don't wanna hear none of that 'Cornbread Red dumped me' bullshit."

"You won't."

"All right, you're in."

Norman proved to be a formidable Nine-Ball player. They played through the night with the score going back and forth. Spectators and bettors drifted away one by one until only a few were left. At one point, Red was six games down and had to reach deep within himself to pull it back to even. At ten in the morning, when they agreed to take a break, he was five games up.

Red picked up a corned beef sandwich at a joint next door and ate it as he and Al walked the two blocks to his hotel room. "How we doing?" he asked between bites.

"Well, right now it looks like a lot of work for a small piece of cheese. You got to play him a little tighter, Cornbread—keep him off the table."

"Yeah, I got to get my break working."

"That's right," Al said. "He's killing your momentum every time he gets to the table. It's like starting over cold every time you get up."

Red stopped him with a hand on his arm. "You covering any side action?"

"No."

"You oughta," Red said. "He's gonna be coming apart in a couple a hours. I've seen it a million times. If I had

him on a snooker table, he'd a *gone off* already. Don't you
see how he's getting sloppy going into the corner—hitting
the long rail?"

"No, Red, I hadn't noticed."

"Look, go on back and do what you can to press the
action. See if you can get him up to six or seven-hundred
a game."

The color drained from Al's face. "I don't know,
Cornbread, I don't know if that's the right—"

"Look here, goddamn it. If you don't know what the
hell to do, listen to someone who does." Red's voice was
strong and cutting, the same tone he had used in the
carnivals to get the mark to take the big bet.

Al hesitated for only a second. "Okay, Cornbread, I'll
take care of it." He turned and headed back to Sarge's.

In his room, Red took a quick shower and laid on the
bed with his feet on the pillows. As the blood flowed to
his brain, he closed his eyes and rubbed his temples. After
ten minutes, he got up and put on a pair of casual pants
and a fresh shirt and left the room.

Back at the barber shop, he got the shave and hot
towel as planned. He tipped the shoeshine boy five dollars
for buffing his alligators and returned to the pool table.
Norman was already there pocketing balls.

As Red predicted, Norman's game fell apart. It didn't
happen, however, in two, four, or even six hours. A full
eight hours later, he missed a *dog* two-ball in the side—
and boom—it was like taking the plug out of an oil pan.
Within twenty minutes, Norman's engine had seized up
and Red put nine more beads on his side of the wire. He

and Al were up seventy-five hundred when Norman's
backer quit.

Red paid the four-hundred-dollar table bill and tipped
Sarge an extra hundred for the shave. He bought a box of
Havanas from a guy and passed them out to anyone who
wanted one. Norman, slumped in a chair, refused the one
offered to him. Red smoked half of his before snubbing it
out and going back to his room. He slept for fourteen
hours, woke up, and smoked the other half before heading
back to Detroit.

Sometimes after a player gets badly mangled, he steers
clear of the guy who beat him—he accepts the defeat.
Other times, the beaten man practices and reworks his
strategy until he regains his belief in himself and then he
sets up a rematch. Sometimes, the beaten man refuses
altogether to admit he was *really* beaten. He blames this
condition or that, and as soon as he gets his money good,
he wants to play again.

Red didn't know where Norman was coming from
when he called a few weeks later, but he agreed to return
to Benton Harbor. Three days later he was in the Apollo
Bar, this time with two Detroit friends, and a ten-thousand
dollar bankroll.

"I'll give you the break, Norman," Red said, giving
his toughest stare. A spot that big to a player of Norman's
caliber was tantamount to an insult.

"Don't need it, Red. I'll play you for five-hundred a
set, seven games to a set. All I want from you is the
eight." He was standing face to face with Cornbread.

"You're feeling so confident," Red said, "give me the break." There was a titter from the other people around the bar who were listening in on the conversation. Red smiled, delighted to get the response he had anticipated.

"It's pay as you play, Cornbread. No wire."

"All right, let's go."

They walked across the street to Sarge's. There was already a hubbub of bet making and other excited conversation coming from the back room. Red said hello to Sarge, who was finishing a customer in the barber chair, and went into the poolroom. There was close to fifty people and a palpable excitement in the small room. As Red was screwing his cue together, he saw Don Alabaster sitting with a group of men and waved him over.

"Hey, Al. Come 'ere," he said.

The thin man came over to the table. "Hello, Cornbread."

"You want to get in on this action with me, Al?"

"I'm gonna pass, Cornbread. I've been watching Norm for the last two weeks and he's been playing like a god. Absolutely unbelievable." He looked up at Red and their eyes met for the briefest of seconds before he looked away. "Fact of the matter is, Red, I'm backing Norm in this match."

Red couldn't believe his ears. He could feel the blood rushing to his face and struggled to control the rising anger. "I can't believe it, man. I win you four-thousand dollars the last time I'm here and you're gonna bet against me?" He shook his head. "That's a shit thing to do."

Al paled and took a short step backwards. "Hey man," he said, "I got to take care of my own interest."

Red crushed his cigarette out in the ashtray. "You deserve to get busted."

"You might be in for a surprise."

Red grabbed a handful of balls from the corner pocket and threw them on the table. They bounced loudly and rolled to the far end. As Red moved to clear the side pocket of balls, Al turned and walked back to his friends.

They began to play—and it was true—Norman was in excellent shape. He was playing effortlessly, all of his movements flowing with an easy rhythm. Every time he got to the table, he ran out. The few times he didn't run out, he was refusing the tough, aggressive shots he had taken in their first match, and was playing safe instead. His shot selections and strategic moves were faultless. Red was not getting a chance to stretch out. Every time he came to the table, he was presented with a tough kick or a low percentage shot.

By early afternoon, Red had completely lost control of his temper. He was throwing the balls on the table while racking, slamming the wooden rack on the table bed, and swearing loudly. None of this seemed to bother the other man. At one point, Red threw the cue ball, like a baseball, at the wall. It smashed through a framed picture of Minnesota Fats, penetrating the plaster and falling down inside the wall. Play stopped when they couldn't agree on which replacement cue ball to use. Finally, Sarge kicked a hole in the wall and retrieved the original.

"This is bullshit!" Red screamed a few minutes later. He threw his cue stick on the table. "I can't play for this chicken feed—put some goddamn real money up, motherfucker!"

"You wanna play pool, Cornbread?" Norman dragged out the name with a sarcastic whine. "I'll play you pool. Whatever you got, put it up!"

"Play me even." Red said.

"You want the eight back? You got it. I don't need anything to kick your ass. Talk to your backers, Cornbread—show me this big game you're mouthing off about."

Red conferred with the two men he had brought with him from Detroit. After a moment, he came back to the table and threw a roll of cash on it. "Seven-thousand—a race to fifteen—winner take all." He leaned against the table and watched as Norman talked with Al.

They asked Sarge to hold the stake money and flipped for the break. Red won, and without hesitation, broke the balls. The seriousness of the increased stakes brought a keener edge to his game. It was just as he figured it would be. He always played better when the stakes were raised, and most other people did not. It was almost always a good move for him to press the stakes. He had beaten a lot of good players like that.

When Norman finally got a sinkable shot, he capitalized on it and ran two racks. In his third rack, he played perfect shape on the four-ball which was frozen on the rail an inch down from the side pocket. The lay of the balls required him to roll the four past the side pocket and down to the corner. He undercut it by a hairbreadth and the four hit the point of the side pocket and bounced out into the middle of the table. Red got up and ran four racks.

Control of the game went back and forth. Each man would put together a string of two or three wins and then screw up. After about an hour of this, Cornbread was *on the hill*. He only needed one more win to take the match. Norman needed two games and it was Red's break.

Red was feeling confident—he was in control and knew it. He was playing totally on instinct—moving fast with little conscious thought. He came to the table after Norman racked the balls and set the cue ball about four inches to the left of the head spot. He eased into his breaking stance, stroked twice, and let it fly. The cue ball hit the one-ball full in the face and caromed straight up in the air. People said later, that if it wasn't for the light hanging over the table, it would have hit the ceiling. As it was, the cue smacked into the fluorescent fixture and both cue ball and bulb fell to the table and landed in the midst of the still expanding rack of balls.

There was a split second of silence before every man was on his feet—filling the room with an uproar of amazement and wonder. Cornbread walked over to the side rail, picked up the cube of chalk, and calmly chalked his stick. After about a minute, people began to quiet down and take their seats. Several were lighting cigarettes. Red was smiling.

"Holy shit," someone noticed. "The nine went in!"

Pandemonium broke loose. People jumped to their feet; drinks fell to the floor. People laughed and slapped each other on the back. Everybody was trying to talk at once. One guy, who had a bet on Red, threw the money he was holding into the air. Even the people who had bet against him could not contain their delight.

Al grabbed at the sleeve of the man next to him. "It's no good—it's no good!" he cried. When that man pushed him aside, he tried to get the attention of another. "It doesn't count!" he whined. "He hit the light. It's no good."

Fifteen minutes later people were still talking about it. Sarge ruled that since the light was part of the playing equipment, and the cue ball never left the field of play— the shot was legal. He told Al to shut up and gave the stake money to Red.

Everybody went across the street to the Apollo. Although he had been drinking heavily since his carnival days, Red didn't particularly enjoy going to bars. The nature of his profession required a certain amount of time in bars, but usually after he had a game set up, or located whoever it was he had been looking for, he left. He was much more comfortable in pool halls.

He sat at one of the tables with his two friends and one of the locals who had bet on him. They were drinking shots of Crown Royal, and washing them down with beer. Every couple of minutes, someone else was coming up to the table to congratulate him on his win and his incredible break shot. Red responded to the attention with rare form—he was jovial and witty.

Al put on a short apron when he came in, and moved behind the bar to assist the bartender with the unexpected crowd. When the demand for drinks slowed down a bit, he came over to Red's table.

"I should never have let him give you back the eight," he said.

"If the bear hadn't stopped to take a piss, the hunter wouldn't of shot 'im," Red said. The men at the table laughed.

"I mean it, Cornbread, he'd a won if he'd a kept the eight."

Red set his mug down, looked up into Al's face, and spoke. "You got another seven-thousand, Al?"

Al looked down at the floor and shook his head.

"Well, why don't you just get your apron back behind that counter and get us another round here." He motioned to include the men at the table with him.

"I need that money, Cornbread, you gotta give me a chance to win it back."

"I'd be happy to, Al. Maybe some of these people in here think you know something about pool. Maybe they'll put up the cash for you." There was more laughter.

Al puffed up his chest and stood a little straighter. "I'll put my bar up against the seven-thousand."

"The bar?" Red said. "What the hell am I gonna do with a bar?"

"I know it's not much," Al said, "but it makes money."

Red laughed. "You think I'm gonna come in here and put that little apron on and run drinks to people?"

"If you win, you could hold the bar as my marker. I'd pay you."

"Sure you would."

"Give me a chance, Cornbread."

Red thought about it. In pool circles it was considered a mark of respect to accept all challenges. You *had heart* if you were willing to play until your opponent was busted and he *had heart* if he could *take the heat*. Red considered it foolish and ill-advised for Al to pursue this wager, but he respected his determination.

"You gonna stay with your man this time, Al?"

Al was silent.

"You own the building?"

"No, I've got a lease."

"I'll put up five-thousand against your bar."

"It's worth more than that, Cornbread."

"Not to me it's not," Red said.

Red was slightly flushed from the whiskey and the earlier win, and played like a man under no pressure at all. He knew he was going home a winner whatever the outcome. Norman was dragging badly and although he put up a valiant effort, he just did not have the resources left. The match was over quickly.

Back at the Apollo, the mood was somber. People were quiet. Al's crushing loss seemed to strike a chord within them all. Red cracked a few jokes in an attempt to regain the earlier atmosphere, but it was futile.

"This is my bar," he said, "and I'm buying a round for the house."

His two friends from Detroit and a couple of others gave a lukewarm hurrah, but most of the patrons merely raised their glasses or remained silent. Several refused the offered drinks completely.

It was a common practice among the hustling fraternity to give a busted player some *out-of-town money*—a small sum to find another game with, a chance to rebuild his bankroll. Red had been on both sides of this exchange many times and the value of the custom was very clear to him. Once in Fulton, he had won a small photography stand from a local businessman and in a moment of graciousness and practicality, had given it back to him for a promise of sixty dollars. The guy continued to make a living and Red continued to win from him.

"Look here," he said when Al came to his table. "I'm a pool player. I don't want your bar. Owe me two-thousand and we'll call it even."

Al sat down—relieved. A few people started talking.

"And one last thing," Red said, "don't you ever take my money in here."

"Your money is no good here," the thin man agreed emphatically.

"Good. Give everybody here whatever they want!"

Two weeks later, at a Detroit room, one of Red's friends who was in Benton Harbor came and sat next to him.

"Man, I bet you're glad you didn't take that bar from Alabaster." he said.

"What do you mean?" Red said.

His friend answered. "Didn't you hear?"

"No—what?"

"Two guys came in and robbed the joint last night."

"No shit," Red said.

"Al's dead—shot right in the head."

12

FAME

That summer was a time of unrest in the big cities of the United States. In Detroit, the balance of economic and political power was shifting with the same sureness as the shifting of the continental plates—the unstoppable power versus the immovable obstacle. Something had to give.

Red, one pointed as always, and oblivious to social conditions, was on his way with Beryl to a poolroom deep inside one of the black neighborhoods. It was no big deal for Red. He was comfortable around pool players and poolrooms wherever they were. In the pool world, status was awarded only for the ability to play. Color, race, and social standing were unimportant. Red was the same loud-mouth wild man in the black rooms as he was in the white.

"Hey!" he shouted as they came in the room. "Any of you black motherfuckers want to play some fifty dollar Nine-Ball?"

There was dead silence in the room. The eyes of twenty or thirty black men fixed on Red and Beryl. "Is that you, Cornbread?" a voice piped up from the back of the room. It was Brooklyn Charlie. "Man, you crazy."

Charlie came up to talk with them and the other men went back to their games.

"It's a bad night to be here, Red," Charlie said.

"What do you mean?"

"Man, there's a lot of tension around here. The cops just busted a speak-easy a couple blocks from here—people are tight—a lot of the brothers have gone over there."

"I don't care about that bullshit. Let's play Nine-Ball. I'll give you the eight."

They racked and broke the balls. Halfway through the rack there was the sound of a siren—then two—then three. Then came the sound of gunfire—close by. Red went with the others to the front door and looked around. It was hot and sticky; a windless summer night. When a cop car, and then another, came careening around the corner with lights flashing and sirens screaming, the men retreated back into the poolroom. Charlie and Red returned to their table.

"I think I'm gonna get on home, Cornbread," Charlie said. He started unscrewing his cue stick.

"Let's at least finish the set," Red said. Before Charlie could answer, there was the sound of cars out front—sudden braking and tires squealing—the slam of car doors and loud voices. Three or four guys inside the poolroom bolted for the back door. The front door burst open and a wave of blue uniforms and night sticks spread into the room.

"This place is closed. Everybody's going home. Right now." It was a big, broad shouldered duty sergeant speaking.

"Hey, man. We got a game going on here," Red said. "Let us finish."

The sergeant walked directly up to Red. He stopped about four inches from his face, and pressed the butt end of a night stick up against his belly just above the belt. Red could smell his aftershave. "Get the fuck out of here," the cop whispered ominously. "Right now."

Red waved Beryl over and they left by the front door. Outside, there was a smattering of gunfire a few blocks away. They could see the flashing lights from police cars reflected on the tall building at the end of the block. They got in Beryl's car and headed north. Beryl took the first left and then a right. There were angry people on the sidewalks and the sounds of glass being broken. When something that sounded like a rock hit the car, they realized the seriousness of the situation—Beryl hit the gas—made another left and then a quick right. On the left was a building on fire; a mob of people in front of it pulling clothes out of the broken storefront. Down the block on the other side of the street, flames poured out of the second-story windows of an apartment building.

"Holy shit," Beryl exclaimed. The street they were on was a boulevard. There was an island dividing the opposing lanes. Theirs was the only moving car in sight. Up ahead, the street came to a dead end as it veered to go around an ancient church. The church's twin steeples were outlined by the night sky and the angry flames climbing from its lower roof. The street was blocked by a crowd of people. To the left of the church was a car, upside down and afire. They were trapped.

"Over the curb, man! Over the curb!" Red shouted.

Beryl yanked on the steering wheel—the front end bounced high as the car hit the curb—once again as the muffler and back wheels slammed against the concrete and onto the grass. They clipped a small tree with the right rear fender—fishtailed to the left—caught another tree on the driver's side and were thrown onto the pavement going the opposite way. Beryl pressed the accelerator to the floor.

"Motherfucker!" Red yelled. Beryl ran the stop light at the corner and threw the car into a turn and onto Michigan Avenue heading north. They were at the city limits when the dragging muffler finally let go.

The riot effectively closed the city down. The National Guard was called in and even the suburbs established and enforced a curfew. Red, almost broke, decided it was a good time to go to Tampa and get his poolroom "investment" back. He got Kilroy, who had been there before, to go with him.

They got the money back without a hassle—about thirty-five hundred. "Let's take this and blaze a path through the poolrooms of Florida that won't no one ever forget!" Red said. They partied that night at a joint Kilroy knew and made their plans.

The next morning, Red woke ready to go, but found Kilroy in a bad way. He was sick—delirious—vomiting—talking nonsense. Red, alarmed, went for a doctor. Outside of the obvious symptoms, the doctor could find nothing wrong. He suggested bed rest and a light diet.

For two months, Red stayed and took care of Kilroy—paying for the room, for food, and for a nurse to come by a couple of times a week. By the middle of September, he was strong enough for Red to send home. Red, himself, caught a bus back to Detroit.

Two days before the Johnston City tournament, a writer from the Detroit Free Press tracked Red down in a poolroom on the west side. "Are you going to the Hustler's Tournament?" he wanted to know.

"I will if I can get a ride," Red replied.

The writer offered to supply the ride if Red took him along for the story. Red agreed and they left that day.

They made a stop in Anderson, Indiana, and picked up a backer, a small time *money man,* that Red knew. They made another stop in Marion to play a local hustler and in the morning, they cruised into Johnston City.

It was a normal tournament, not much different than the year before, or the year before that. There were lots of reporters and TV people milling around—snooping out the color, the story. The gambling and the *wolfing* were in high style as always. Red thought nothing about it when the Free Press writer left for home on the third day. He'd see the paper later—no big deal.

Back in Detroit, a few weeks later, Red was shocked when the story came out. His picture was the full front page of the "Detroit" magazine—delivered with every one of a couple million Sunday newspapers. The caption on the front page read: "CORNBREAD RED: The Saga of Our Greatest Pool Player." Inside was a detailed ten-page story—with pictures. A full spread. Red was famous.

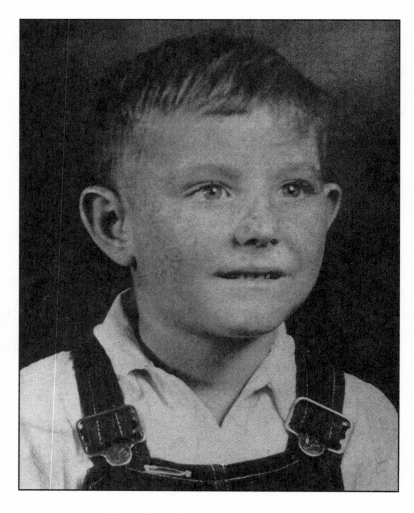

RED GETS A HAIRCUT 1938

(unknown)

IN THE "PIT" AT JOHNSTON CITY 1967
(unknown)

DETROIT

Seer Jeane Dixon's
Detroit Forecast

Sunday

The Beautiful Girls
Of the Auto Show

The Magazine of Michigan's Metropolis   December 1, 1968   The Detroit Free Press

CORNBREAD RED: The Saga of Our Greatest Pool Hustler

"DETROIT" MAGAZINE 1968

(Detroit Free Press)

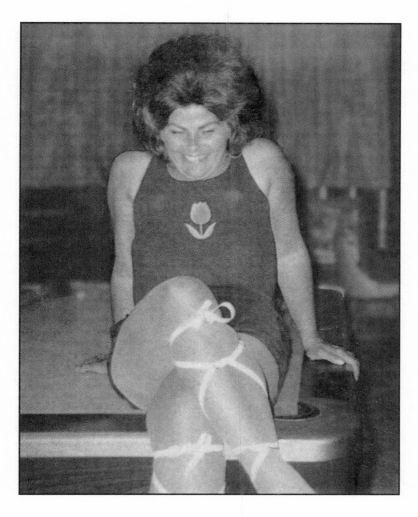

BERNIE IN "SNAKE SHOES" 1970

(unknown)

HANGING OUT AT THE "RACK" 1979

(unknown)

IN THE "DETROIT NEWS" 1988

(Detroit News)

THE FAMILY AT RED'S BIRTHDAY PARTY 1992

(K.Henning)

13

THE BUST

Being a celebrity was nothing like Red had imagined. All the fears about not being able to get a game were unfounded. It was exactly the opposite—people came out of the woodwork looking for him. Many were amateurs—bankers, businessmen, doctors, and lawyers. Plumbers, painters, electricians and teachers. All of them wanting to go back to their VFW's and country clubs and brag to their friends, "Yeah, I played that Cornbread Red—"

Sometimes Red had to give up a *little weight*, as pool players called a handicap, but these players were unsophisticated. They didn't know whether they were getting a good game or not. The amateur action was easy, and so was the money.

Inside the hustler culture, however, it was a different story. As *top dog*, Red was the target for every hot-to-trot shooter working his way up the food chain. This action was tough and serious. It was head to head—heart to heart—dog eat dog—and survival of the fittest. Red ducked no one. He met all comers head on.

The *wolfing,* or haggling, became more evolved and crucial. It determined the game, the game determined the money, and the money determined who survived. Everything winnowed down to the last few best gamblers and Red was one of them. He survived and won respect in the process because it was so clear he *wanted to win*. It meant something to him. There was no ambiguity about it—he was angry when he lost.

Fats came to town and Red played him One-Pocket on the east side. When the room closed down late that night, they were still playing. "Come on, Fats. I know another place we can go." They drove to the "Achilles Heel" where the match continued in the back room. Fifteen or twenty men who were *sweating,* or betting on, the match followed them over.

Sometime after four in the morning, the owner brought a big plate of sandwiches in and everyone took a break. Fats grabbed a sandwich with each hand and sat down. "I gotta quit, Cornbread. You busted me."

"You gonna give me the last two-hundred?" Red asked.

"Ain't got it," He took a big bite out of a baloney sandwich. "Give me five-hundred to get back home with."

Red knew about Fats' reputation as a *bite* man. He was famous for getting people to give him money when he was supposedly broke. There was a story going around about one pool player giving him a hundred a day to eat on for over two weeks. When he heard that Fats had lost two-grand in a craps game, the player realized he'd been taken, and went after Fats to punch him in the nose—only to end up giving him another hundred. Red, who had a huge desire not to be known as a sucker, had no intention of giving Fats any *walking money.* "I ain't giving you a dime," he said.

"It ain't right to leave a man busted, Cornbread," Fats said, taking another bite of sandwich.

"I ain't gonna leave you busted, I'm gonna get you a *job.*" Red smiled as he stressed the last word. He got up and walked over to the coke machine where two guys were talking. After a few minutes he came back to the table where Fats was now on his third sandwich.

"See that tall guy?" Red asked. He pointed in the general direction of the coke machine.

"What about him?"

"He's a big wheel at one of them yacht clubs down on the river. He's gonna get you three-hundred to do an exhibition there—tomorrow." Red laughed with delight at the look on Fats' face. He left for home still smiling—it was a great feeling to put one over on the fat man.

About a year later, Titanic Thompson flew Red to Iowa and staked him against a big time corn farmer. They won fourteen-thousand and split it even. Red took a cab all the way to Chicago and a train from there back to Detroit.

He was celebrating in a room downtown, when he got the news that Beryl was in town. He borrowed a car and drove down to the Cass Corridor to look for him. The Corridor had gone down hill pretty quick since the heyday of the Hole. It looked rougher—a few more prostitutes, a few more drunks. There were several vacant buildings—testimony to the riot three years earlier.

When Red pulled up in front of Beryl's favorite bar on Third Avenue, he noticed an unmarked police car out in front. There was an "x" on the license plate. Red looked through the driver's window. There was a pair of riot shotguns in holders and a lot of other equipment inside. It was one of the cars used by the famous "Big Four" units. These were cars loaded with four officers—all big, all tough—assigned to the worst street crime areas, and given a lot of leeway to get the job done. Red hesitated for a second and then went into the building.

One of the "Big Four" was leaning against the bar and looked at Red as the light from the open door illuminated his entry. As the door swung closed and the room darkened, Red saw another officer leaning over the bar in serious conversation with the bartender. Two others were flanking Beryl who was pressed up against the wall. Even from where he was standing, Red could see that he was a mess. His eyes were bloodshot, his hair messed up, and his clothes rumpled. He looked like he hadn't shaved for two or three days.

"What's going on?" Red asked, stepping into the center of the room. He was trying his best to look calm. The big cop at the bar moved to intercept him.

"Cornbread!" Beryl exclaimed. "Tell these guys who I am. Tell 'em I'm not a stick up man."

The big cop was in front of Red. "You know this guy?" he asked.

"I know him," Red replied.

"Are you Cornbread Red?" interrupted one of the other cops—the youngest one.

"That's what they call me."

The young cop turned to the big one. "He's one of the best pool players in the world. I read about him in the paper."

"Oh, yeah?" the big one said, not impressed at all. "Who's your friend here, Cornbread?"

"That's Beryl, he's a pool player, too."

"He fits the description of an armed robbery suspect."

"It ain't him," Red said with conviction, "the only robbin' this boy has ever done was with a cue stick."

The big cop looked at Red for a moment and then waved the others over to the bar. They conferred for a couple of minutes before the youngest came back. "We're gonna let your friend go," he said, "but you better get him out of here and clean him up. He stinks."

"I'll do that officer," Red said. The cops left. When the dimness of the bar settled back in, Red turned to Beryl. "Man, you look a mess."

"All right, all right," Beryl acknowledged, "I been out for a few days."

"You look it. Come on, let's go."

As they walked to the borrowed car Red asked him, "Where you been?"

"All over. I ran into Fats in a joint down river. I ga—"

"Fats? What'd you mean Fats?" Red interrupted.

"He's in town," Beryl repeated. "You should of seen him. Dressed to the nines and driving a brand new Lincoln. Tol' me to tell you thanks."

"What?"

"He said that yacht club you fixed him up with had him back. He said they gave him that new Lincoln."

The next day Red was in a foul mood. He spent most of the day sprawled in front of the television, eating potato chips and drinking beer while Beryl slept.

When he woke up, Red took him to the Rack, a medium-sized room located in Oak Park, a predominately Jewish suburb of Detroit. It was in a square cinder block building—one large room with a tile floor and a twelve-foot ceiling. There were twenty-four tables, all Brunswick Anniversaries with curved corners and mahogany sides.

Gil, the owner, was a big, soft-spoken man. For many of the pool players, particularly the younger ones, he was the proverbial Jewish Mother—someone to tell your troubles to—to get advice from. Someone who would cash a check for a broke player and hold it until he was flush again. He was an all-around good guy, who loved the game and the action.

Red started hanging out there because Gil was quick to overlook outward displays of gambling. It made it easier to make a living, and besides—Gil knew a lot of rich Jews who liked to gamble. Most of the other hustlers in town followed Red over there. It was now one of the main action spots in town.

"Wow!" Beryl said when he found out how much Red had won in Iowa. "What the hell are we doing here? Let's go get a bottle and a couple of hookers."

"Naw, I'm tired of that crap," Red said. They were sitting in the little snack area. Red was slumped in his chair. He waved his hand to include the entire poolroom. "I'm tired of *all* this crap."

"You should be happy you got a pocket full of money."

"Here—you take it. I don't even want it." He held a fat roll out to Beryl.

"You're talkin' crazy, Cornbread. Come on, let's get some action going in here."

"I mean it," Red said, "I wish I never took the game up." He looked up at Beryl, now standing. "I don't like the game anymore, and you know why? Cause everybody thinks a pool player is a bum. They think you're a bum no matter how *good* you get. I'm sick of it."

"It's just a game, Red."

"Nobody appreciates a pool player. Nobody respects how hard we work on it or what we have to give up for it. They think we're doing the same thing they do when they're knocking a bunch a balls around without a lick of sense."

"You're taking it too serious, Red. Just have a good time and be happy you're shooting good."

"I saw Nixon on TV yesterday. All those reporters calling him Mr. President—everybody dressed up in suits. He couldn't run a rack if you put 'em in front of the pockets." Red got to his feet. "I'm going home, Beryl. Keep that money and gamble with it for me—I'll get it back later."

Red didn't make it back to the Rack for four days, and then, only because Beryl called to tell him about some out-of-town action setting up. A nineteen-year-old hotshot from the other side of the state was in the Rack with a *stakehorse*, a big mouth, and a big bankroll. Red, who liked this player, reluctantly got off the sofa and took a cab there.

The parking lot was full of cars. Just to the left of the door, three guys were pitching pennies against the wall for three-hundred-and-fifty a throw. Red stopped and watched for a few minutes. It was warm for the first of May and both of the front doors were wide open to let the breeze circulate. Red stepped inside and saw about a hundred people and a lot of different games in process. Within a few minutes, he was back into the flow of things—wolfing with a half dozen different gamblers— boasting and bragging—daring them to take a shot at him.

"Where you been, Red?" asked Fat Art.

"I been booked up on the TV," Red answered. "How's the kid doing?"

Fat Art looked at the nineteen-year-old player. "He hasn't really got into anything heavy yet. Frank's been chasing him around for about an hour." Art nodded toward a big man dressed in an expensive business suit, now approaching the kid.

Frank Bryce had been a fixture around Detroit poolrooms for years. He was at least six-foot-two—big boned with a booming voice and huge hands. Red had seen him win money from people who didn't believe he could hold six pool balls in one of them. If he had pursued weight lifting, Red thought, he would have been a champion. As it was, he was just shy of playing world-class pool.

Red and Art watched as the kid fenced with Frank. Both of them were talking bold, but neither was getting pinned down. They were still feeling it out. The kid glanced toward Red and saw him for the first time. He held a finger in the air to tell Frank to hold it, and walked over to Red.

"Hey, Cornbread, how are you doing?"

"I'm all right."

"You're good at match-ups, Red. Can I play Frank eight to six? Can I win?"

Red was shocked by such a breach of hustler protocol. He was used to being asked for advice, but never in front of others. He kept a poker face and looked at Fat Art.

"I got to get something to eat, Art. I'll see you later." He turned and walked toward the snack area, completely ignoring the younger player.

A little while later, Red was able to pull him aside.

"Listen," he said, "don't ever ask me in front of someone else who's gonna win if you play so-and-so. You're putting me in an awkward position."

"Come on, Red, I don't know how this guy plays. You gonna let me get killed out there or what?"

"No, I'll help you, but don't be a fool about it—show some sense. Look, all you got to do is to come up to me and say 'Hey, Red, I'm thinking about playing so-and-so for such-and-such. Want to get in on it?' If I say no, you'll know what I think about it."

"I'm gonna play him snooker for six-hundred a game," the kid said. "You want to keep score for ten-percent?"

"All right," Red said.

Snooker was one of Red's favorite games. It was played on a ten-foot table with small balls and tight pockets. The pockets were designed to kick a ball out unless it was precisely hit. It was a game that tolerated *no* slop. What Red liked even more than snooker was One-Pocket *on* a snooker table. He was probably the best in the world at it.

Keeping score was easy. There was a wire strung along the side of the overhead light fixture that had about a hundred little wooden *beads* strung on it. At the end of each player's inning, Red would reach up with the end of a cue stick and slide beads from one side to the other to keep track of the number of points, if any, the player scored during his inning. The main function of a scorekeeper was to keep it honest—to eliminate arguments.

The game was going smoothly and Red had an opportunity to look around the room for Beryl. There were a lot of people there, most of them gamblers, and most of them people that he knew. There were several older men sitting at the snack bar that Gil referred to, in private, as the "Millionaire Jews." Red had already gambled with a couple of them.

In the back of the room, "Bugs" from Chicago was playing another black player. He was one of the best bankers in the world. It was tough to ever *lock him up*, or keep him hooked, because he could always bank his way out of it. A player was *hooked* if either the cue ball or the object ball was hidden and the required shot couldn't be made. When Bugs was hooked, he would simply bank the ball off of one, two, three, four, or even five rails to get a legal hit.

The kid whooped when he made the seven-ball and Red's attention was drawn back to the snooker table. He moved the whole string of beads to the right and set the balls up for a new game.

After the break, Frank and the kid played safeties back and forth for what seemed, to Red, to be ten minutes. In snooker, a player is not required to hit a rail after contacting the required ball and this sometimes resulted in mind boggling defensive play—tiny move after tiny move. Red's attention wandered around the room again.

Two tables away, a man he didn't know hit on One-eyed Pete for a game. Pete suggested a game of Nine-Ball for five dollars. The stranger agreed and went to a cue stick rack by the front door, and examined a cue. Red was about to look away, when the stranger made a funny move. He glanced quickly around the room, moved to the open front door, and made a sweeping motion with his arm.

"What the—?" Red said out loud.

The side door smashed open. Twenty or thirty cops, with helmets and visors, burst into the room. Another group, about the same size, were through the front door by the time Red looked back. They were wearing uniforms with the pant legs tucked into their boots. They were carrying guns and riot sticks.

There was a great reaction from the crowd. Several dropped to the ground on instinct, and scrambled to get under the pool tables. A whole bunch of them put their hands up in the air. Two of the "Millionaire Jews" at the snack bar fainted and fell to the floor. Red was stunned.

A cop with a bull horn forced his voice over the pandemonium. "This is a raid!" he yelled. "Everybody put your hands on your head and back up to the wall!" The cops formed a line and moved in unison to force the men toward the back wall. "I repeat: this is the South Oakland County Tactical Support Unit. This is a police raid. Put your hands on your head and move to the wall. Face the wall with your hands on your head."

There were recognizable signs of relief from several of the men. "Fuck!" Frank Bryce shouted in disgust. "It's the fuckin' cops! I thought it was a fuckin' hit—a fucking St. Valentine's Day hit." Two of the cops told him to shut up and poked him with riot sticks until he moved with the others toward the back wall. Red went along without coaxing.

When they got everything under control, the police confiscated all the big money bank rolls. Frank Bryce was relieved of a sizable hunk, as was the kid's backer. All the men were frisked for weapons—none were found. The police brought in a fingerprint team and a pair of photographers and set them up at one end of the room. They lined the patrons up alongside a row of pool tables and moved them through like an assembly line—mug

shots and prints. Red joked with the cops and tried to read
the insignia on their uniforms. They were from Oak Park
and at least seven other neighboring cities. After he was
fingerprinted, Red looked around the room. Gil was by
the front counter, sitting in handcuffs and looking totally
forlorn. Past him, two guys in white coats attended the
two collapsed men by the snack counter. Red could see
the ambulance through the open front doors. Beyond it,
were two official looking buses. In a surprisingly short
time, Red, and the other ninety-seven men were
processed, loaded onto the buses, and on their way to the
Oakland County Jail.

At the jail, the men were lined up again to turn in
personal property before being assigned to a cell. Red
turned in his wallet, his keys, and seven cents—his entire
bankroll. Thank God I gave that money to Beryl, he
thought, as he looked around at the twenty-or-so men in
the cell with him. Everyone was milling around, trying to
bum cigarettes from the few who had them, and
speculating about what would happen next. Three men
were already asleep alongside the far wall. Red moved up
to the cell door and leaned on the single horizontal bar
with his elbows and watched as a guard escorted the next
batch of prisoners in. Chicago Bugs was one of them.
"Hey, Bugs!" Red yelled as the black player stepped into
a cell, "bank your way outa this one!"

Everyone was released the next morning. Gil was
charged with running a gambling establishment and Red
and ninety-five others were charged with frequenting one.

Frank Bryce and the kid were both charged with winning at gambling—something Red found ludicrous. "How can two guys who are gambling both be charged with winning?" he asked a reporter who tracked him down for the story. "Ain't but one of them gonna win."

"What about the forty-two-thousand dollars the police confiscated?" the reporter asked.

"Don't people have a right to pack money on them?" Red asked. "There were millionaires in there and a lot of real wealthy people. Some people like golf. Others like pool. Sure they bet. Name one sport where the betting ain't heavy."

The reporter ignored his challenge. "How come there were so many people in there, Cornbread?" he asked.

"I was supposed to play an exhibition match," Red said. "When the word gets out I'm gonna play, the place always gets crowded." He took a drag on his cigarette and blew out the smoke. "I'm liable to draw people. Just like Minnesota Fats."

14

HANGING ON

The aftermath of the big bust was settled quickly. The judge came to the poolroom and the undercover cop testified where each person was when the alleged gambling took place. The only case that stood up to the judge's examination was One-eyed Pete's. He fined him twenty-five dollars for playing the cop for five. All the other cases were dropped.

Gil was delighted even though his license remained suspended. He upped the ante and convinced the two "Millionaire Jews" who fainted to file a lawsuit against the city. They got a hotshot attorney and sued for millions.

This did nothing to improve Red's flagging spirit. With the Rack closed down, there was no *arena* for the action to develop. He went around to different rooms, but there was little happening and he didn't have the will or energy to make it happen. He was almost forty, and the life of a pool player was losing its luster. He felt trapped and hopeless.

That fall, he went to one of the big tournaments, but his heart wasn't in it. He did poorly in tournament play, and not much better in the back room. A magazine sent a photographer and a writer to do a story on the hustlers and

Red overheard them talking with the promoter. They were standing at the bar watching the players gamble in the adjoining room. "Look at all those animals in there—" the promoter said, referring to the players, "all of them trying to get over on each other." It angered Red that the man, who made money off the players, would talk like that about them.

Red didn't make it into the magazine story, and even worse, he got busted. For the first time in nine years of going to tournaments, he was flat broke. He tried to borrow gas money from the promoter and was turned down flat. "I don't loan money to pool players," he was told.

"Screw you and screw your tournament," Red said. He borrowed money from another player and drove back to Detroit.

A few months later, he was inspecting a pool table with Kilroy. Red stroked the cue ball, lying a few inches in front of the corner pocket, and sent it three rails around the table—*snick, snick, snick.* It rolled right up to the edge of the opposite pocket and stopped. "This table runs true," he said.

"Well, it's the only one, Red. These other ones are all messed up."

"It don't matter as long as you know what they'll do," Red said. They were in the Rack. Gil and the "Millionaires" had held the city's feet to the fire and won. Gil had settled for a private club license and reopened the Rack. He pulled out half the tables, rearranged the others, and put up a wall running the length of the building. The side without pool tables was now a card room.

"So, how's this *job* thing going for you?" Red asked.

"It's a piece a cake," Kilroy said. He pulled out a pack of Pall Malls and lit one. He was opening up territories for Frank Bryce. Frank had a warehouse in a Detroit suburb where he sold seconds to the public. He bought these slightly damaged goods from department store chains and import houses, and resold them. His latest venture was to take the show on the road.

"You making any money?"

"You better believe it." Kilroy blew out a cloud of smoke. "Ya wanna know how we do it?"

"Sure."

"Frank buys these framed picture sets for about eight bucks. He's got a guy in the warehouse who puts a $89.95 sticker on 'em. He's got all these salespeople taking them into office buildings and doctor offices—places like that. That's what I'm doing." Kilroy paused to take a couple drags off the Pall Mall. "I bring a couple sets in with me. I tell the receptionist and the office girls, 'I was in the neighborhood dropping off a shipment to so-and-so and the warehouse overloaded me. I sure don't want to drive all the way downtown to turn two sets back in. Can you help me out? You can have 'em at cost—forty-five dollars.' They jump on it."

"Sounds easy enough."

"Frank's already got about thirty guys on the road—adding more every day. Mark my words, Cornbread, ole Frank's gonna be a *rich* man."

"I believe it."

"Another thing," Kilroy said. "Watch this place. It's gonna take off like a rocket."

Red nodded in agreement.

Over the next few weeks, Red did what he could to resurrect his passion for the game. He found a little action at the Rack, and did his best to stir up more. He walked in one day and yelled for everyone to hear: "I wanna play some fifty dollar Nine-Ball! I'll give anyone in the joint the seven, the eight, and the break." It was a tremendous offer. He couldn't believe it when no one jumped on it. He went down the line of hustlers who were in that day and asked them name by name. "How 'bout you, Al? No? How 'bout you, Kim?"

"I got no money, Red."

"How about you, Ed?"

"I got to get outa here in a few minutes."

No one would take him up on it. He returned the next day and made the same offer. Finally, George Middleditch, the trick shot artist, stepped forward. He was a dark man, with a thick shock of black hair, thick eyebrows, and a mustache. "I might lose," he said, "but if I don't take you up on this, Cornbread, I'd have to quit the game in shame." They played for the next two weeks—George kept his pride, but lost his money.

It was after one of these games that Red got a call from Beryl. Could Red come and pick him up later that night at a bar on Livernois and Vernor? The Whistlestop? Red agreed. "I'll see you about midnight," he said.

15

BERNIE

Bernie was the baby of the family. As the last of fourteen children, she came late enough to miss the tough times the family had gone through. And with so many brothers and sisters, she became aware of, at an early age, the different courses a person's life could take. One brother was in jail. Another was a minister. Two were in the Air Force and two worked at Great Lakes Steel in Detroit.

They all grew up in Floyd county in eastern Kentucky—in the heart of coal mining country. The family owned the hardware store there and lots of different properties and houses. Her father's response to the lean years of the depression was to spend the next twenty years fathering children and making money. He was very good at both.

He came down with arthritis when Bernie was a young teenager. With the same vengeance he had pursued children and money, he pursued the cure. The family fortune disappeared in a five year flurry of mud baths and healing waters. By the time of his death, all that was left were a few pieces of property that Bernie's mother was forced to sell.

Bernie married, had two kids, and came with her former husband to Detroit back in '56. She was thinking about that as she looked in the mirror. She was getting dressed for a "night out on the town." She laughed—that was a funny way to think about another night at the Whistlestop, the local honky-tonk.

The girl in the full-length mirror laughed back. She was wearing white hotpants, cut as high up the thigh as the law would allow. She laughed again, and bent over to tie the straps on the white snake shoes that were on her feet. Snake shoes had straps that wrapped around and around the calf and tied just below the knee.

She looked in the mirror again and teased her blond hair up a little higher. She bent close to see if any of the light brown roots were showing yet, and was pleased to see they were not. She pulled on a sleeveless, body-hugging top. It was her favorite—a little yellow tulip with two green leaves appliquéd and centered just below the neckline. She looked again and was pleased with what she saw.

She'd been feeling good since the divorce. She had fought it for a long time, for the children's sake, but once it happened, it was like a breath of fresh air; like a springtime breeze blowing through her entire life. She'd had her freedom for over a year now and was still making up for the fun she'd missed while married.

◆   ◆   ◆

When he got to the Whistlestop that night, Red was in baggy jeans and a pair of tennis shoes. He was several weeks overdo for a haircut and two days unshaven. He didn't see Beryl inside, so he got a table in the back and ordered a beer and a shot of Crown Royal. He noticed the girl in the white hotpants almost immediately and was watching her out of the corner of his eye. She was with two girlfriends—all three of them going on and on about this and that. They were having fun—talking and laughing. Three or four times Red watched as men stopped by the girls' table and joked and flirted with them. One bought all three a round of drinks. These girls come in here a lot, he thought.

At one o'clock, Beryl still hadn't shown up and Red found himself hoping that he wouldn't. He could hear the blond girl's voice above the hubbub of the bar and was enjoying it. He didn't want to be interrupted. Her voice was soft and light—with an easy down-home rhythm. He'd bet a hundred she was from Kentucky.

At one-thirty, Beryl was still missing and the girls were on their feet, gathering up their things, and preparing to leave. The blond girl in hotpants glanced at him. He turned his head in embarrassment and stared at the bartender. He felt awkward, even a little shy. He was intensely conscious of his shaggy hair and tired clothes. When he looked back, they were gone.

He went to the door and looked out—there was no sign of them. The bartender yelled for last call and Red went to the bar and ordered another shot of Crown Royal.

"Do those girls come in here often?" he asked.

"Almost every night."

Red took his drink and returned to his table. Just before closing, Beryl finally made it. He was visibly excited. Red waved him over.

"Red—Red—look at this—" he said. "Look at all this money I won." He threw a wad of crumpled bills on the table, pulled some more out of another pocket, and threw those on the table, too. "Look at it, Red—I can't even count it—I don't even know how much I've got."

Red looked at the bills. They were all Canadian singles—there wasn't even fifty dollars there. He looked at Beryl's face—his eyes were glassy—the pupils black and dilated. "What the hell happened to you?" he asked.

"Awwh—Red—" he sat down suddenly and looked at Red—his head swaying back and forth. He looked as if he was going to cry for a second and then broke into a big shit-eating grin. "I was playing this guy and got tired. I asked one of them long-hairs at the bar if he had a pill. He gave me one and I took it. I think it was LSD."

"Oh, no," Red said.

"I only wanted an upper, Red." He shook his head as if trying to wake up. "Man, I been seeing shit all night."

"Here, Beryl, drink the rest of this whisky." Red handed him the glass and Beryl finished it.

"Man, the pool balls had little arms and legs," he said. "They were running all over the table. I couldn't get 'em to listen to me at first, but I finally did. I had 'em jumping in the pocket for me. Any pocket I wanted."

"You better come home with me," Red said.

"When I got to the game ball, I looked at it close. It was the eight-ball. I looked at it again and it had your face on it. You were right there—grinning at me. I smacked you right in the side pocket!"

Red was back the next night—this time with a haircut and a shave. He was wearing a green polyester sport coat he bought in Vegas four years before. The blond was there again and once when he was at the bar ordering, she passed by on the way to her table and said 'hi' to him. He said 'hi' back, but it came out sounding awkward. God, he thought, what the hell's going on with me? He wasn't usually like this with women—usually he was fairly cavalier. He had done okay with the ladies—not anything like Danny Jones, but okay just the same. One girl had even tattooed "Property of Cornbread Red" on one of her breasts. He caught his breath as the blond girl got out of her chair and said good night to her friends. In a moment she was gone.

The next night he was back but she wasn't. The night after that, he got Beryl to come and keep him company. They sat at a table to the side and about two or three tables away from where the girl usually was. By eleven o'clock, when she still hadn't appeared, Beryl suggested they wrap it up and head back to the Rack.

"Let's give her ten more minutes," Red said.

"Well, I'm gonna get another beer then." Beryl walked over to the bar.

Red was feeling a little bit like a sucker—waiting to see a girl he didn't even know. Hell—he'd never even talked with her. "Come on," he said when Beryl came back. "Let's get out of here." As he started to get up, the front door opened. A man in a green tank top came in. Before the door swung closed, Red caught a glimpse of two girls walking up the sidewalk. One of them was the blond girl. "That's her!" he said excitedly.

When they came in, the blond looked toward the back of the room where she had seen Red before. Red thought he saw a frown pass quickly over her face and disappear. She sat down facing her friend with her back to Red and Beryl.

Beryl got up and walked toward them. Red tried to grab his sleeve, but missed. Damn it, he thought. He watched as Beryl put his hands on the table and leaned over to talk. He looked at the other girl as he spoke, and she shook her head when he paused. Beryl laughed and talked some more. He made a motion with his hand toward Red and both girls turned and looked. The blond smiled quickly and turned back around.

Beryl returned to where Red was sitting. "Come on," he said, "we're gonna buy 'em a drink."

Red followed him to the other table. He didn't catch the other girl's name but the blond's was Bernetta.

"Everyone calls me Bernie," she said.

The four of them small talked for a few minutes. "I knew it," Red said when Bernie said she was from Kentucky.

"You've been watching me, haven't you?" she smiled.

"A little bit," Red mumbled. He looked at Beryl for help, but Beryl was talking to the other girl.

"It's all right," Bernie said, "I don't mind."

Beryl stood up. "Come on, Cornbread. Let's take these girls out and show them a good time!"

The other girl laughed. "You don't look like you could show anybody a good time."

"Now, I resent that," Beryl joked. He put his hand in his pocket. "Looky here, girl, I can take you anywhere you want—drinking—dancing—anything." He pulled his hand out and threw a small roll of bills on the table. The one showing was a twenty. "I got enough money for both you girls."

Cornbread pushed his chair back and stood up. He thrust both hands deep into his front pockets and looked at Bernie. With his left hand he dropped a wad of crumpled bills on the table. "I got money, too," he said. He extended his right hand over the table and dropped another bunch of bills and coins. A quarter bounced on its edge, spun easily for a second, wobbled and fell. "I can show you a good time."

"You're looking pretty good," Bernie said.

"They look great!" her friend said. Both girls laughed. They were enjoying themselves. Beryl sat back down.

Red was still standing. When the others noticed, they stopped laughing and looked at him. "Most of my friends are millionaires," he said. He pulled a neatly folded group of bills from his right hip pocket, another bunch from his left, and threw them both on the table.

Bernie jumped to her feet. "Oh, baby!" she laughed, "you're my kind of guy!" She jumped into his arms and kissed him on the cheek.

They went to a restaurant with white tablecloths and waiters. Red refused to let her wipe off the red lipstick still on his cheek. She, on the other hand, refused to call him either Cornbread, Red, or Billy. "I'm going to call you Bill," she said.

After the meal, they ordered cocktails. By the second round, Beryl was in deep conversation with the other girl—Janet—their faces close together. Red and Bernie were free to talk.

"Can I look at your tattoos, Bill?" She reached over and stroked his left arm with her index finger. Red was usually bold and loud when asked about his tattoos. He was embarrassed to have them, but they made him look tough and formidable to prospective competitors. This request by a soft voiced Kentucky girl, however, filled him with a warmth he'd never felt before.

"I got this one when I was working a carnival in St. Louis. Me and this other boy got drunk and we both got these hootchie girls. See, I can make her dance." Red flexed his left forearm and the crudely outlined naked girl moved her hips. He looked at Bernie's face for her reaction.

"Good God," she said softly, "you're X-rated. Have you got any long-sleeve shirts?"

Red laughed and stretched forth his right arm. On the forearm was a skull and crossbones outlined in the same aged and faded blue ink. It was about the size of a half-dollar and was surrounded by four smaller and intricate drawings. Bernie leaned forward to have a closer look, her hair touching Red's cheek. She could make out a woman's face with long flowing hair, a pair of dice showing a three and a four, a musical note, and something that looked like a bottle.

"I got most of this one in Ozark, Alabama." Red said. "This here's for wine, women, song, and gambling. He touched each of the small emblems as he named them.

She whistled lightly. "Have you got any more?"

"An eight-ball on my ankle." He pulled up his pant leg and Bernie leaned over and looked. After a second, she sat up and moved her chair back a couple of inches.

It was an imperceptible move, but Red took note of it. "This is my favorite one," he said hastily. He pushed up his left sleeve and bared the biceps. In the clearest and boldest blue ink was the word *MOTHER*. It was surrounded by a heart.

16

ON THE EDGE

It was a whirlwind romance. They went out the next two nights with Janet and Beryl, and then several nights in a row by themselves. One of Bernie's girlfriends finally spoke to her about it.

"I think you like that redheaded boy," she said.

"I don't like that ole red thing," Bernie replied, but she knew it was true, and it scared her a bit. He was sweet and good to her, but he was also a little rough around the edges. He had money, but she was certain he didn't have a job or a home. Some of the circumstances reminded her of her ex-husband—and she wasn't going through that again.

She brought him home to Melvindale, a suburb of Detroit, and introduced him to her daughter, Sandy, and her son, Greg. His reaction to them—particularly Greg, who had cerebral palsy, was what she had hoped for. They seemed to like him, too. In the next few weeks, he spent more and more time at her home. She liked having him there.

One morning after the kids left for school, they were having coffee at the table in her small kitchen.

"This is getting too serious," she said.

"What do you mean?" he asked.

"You're spending too much time here—I don't know if you should."

"I like being here," Red said.

"I like having you here, too, but I have to be looking down the road a bit, Bill. I've got children—I've got to be thinkin' about the future."

"We could have a future together."

"Can we?"

"Why not?"

"Look at you, Bill. You don't have a roof over your head—you don't have a job. Look at the tattoos on your arms, for godsakes." She was on the edge of tears.

He reached out and took her hand. "I don't want to get hurt again," she said, her voice almost breaking.

Red remembered his mother working at the ammunition factory in Tennessee. He remembered when Thomas came home and became part of the family. "I'm gonna take care of you," Red said. "I'm gonna take care of the kids, too." He felt a great release when he spoke the words. Something wired tight—deep inside himself—gave way. He felt a sense of peace.

"How are you gonna provide for us?" she asked.

"I'll show you."

Red made a few phone calls during the day. After dinner, he put Bernie in the car, closed the door for her, and drove to the Rack. Inside, he introduced her to a few people and escorted her to a seat.

"Sit here," he said. "I'm gonna be playing at this table right here." He pointed to the one in front of them. He left her there with a cup of coffee and went across the room and spoke with a small group of men. A few minutes later he walked to the far end of the poolroom and talked with different men. A few minutes later, he was with yet another group.

Beryl came in, walked over to where she was sitting and gave her a kiss on the cheek. She hadn't seen him in several weeks.

"You doing all right?" he asked.

"Yes."

Red walked up. "You get everything handled?" he asked Beryl.

"Yup. How about you?"

"All set."

Bernie watched as another group of men approached the table. One of them, about Bill's age, placed a thin cue case on the table and pulled his shirt over his head and off. He had a T-shirt underneath.

"That boy used to be a champion," Beryl whispered.

"In what?" she whispered back.

He looked surprised. "In pool," he said, "what do you think?"

"Oh," she said, but she was confused. She had seen her brothers play pool in Kentucky—it just wasn't that big of a deal. She watched as several men gathered around the pool table. The man in the T-shirt was screwing together a pool cue he'd taken from the case. She heard one of the other men call him Evie.

Beryl stood by the snack bar. He pulled an inch-thick stack of bills out of his breast pocket and waved it around like a pork chop. He threw it down on the table where it landed amongst the ketchup and mustard, sugar, and other condiments. "Take a look at that," he said to the men standing there. He walked to the end of the snack bar and ordered a cup of coffee, oblivious to the money left on the table.

"You better pick that up," one of the men said, "before someone walks off with it."

Beryl got his coffee, stopped at the condiments, and picked up both the money and a container of cream. He walked to where Bernie was sitting and set the coffee on the stand next to her.

"Don't let anybody put anything in this," he said. He moved off to the side and she watched as Red and Evie began to play.

"Are you in trouble?" she asked, after Red lost several games in a row.

"I don't think so," Red replied. "We're racing to twenty-one—the first one to get to twenty-one wins. He's only got four games on me."

Bernie had all along suspected this to be a set-up by Red and his friends to impress her. A giant scam to win her over. They talked about big sums of money all the time, but for her it was airy-fairy—the stuff of dreams, and she didn't believe them. She could already hear Bill complaining as they went back to her house without the money. She suspected it was all Beryl's money. The two of them trying to impress her.

She noticed Beryl standing about thirty feet away with three or four other men. They were surrounded by a larger circle of twenty or so. One guy was taking notes on a piece of cardboard torn from an empty candy box. After Evie won the next game and Red had reracked the balls, Beryl called out.

"Come here, Red!" he yelled. "We gonna lay some more money down—take a few more bets. Hey!" he yelled to the man in the T-shirt, who was moving to the table. "*Don't* break those balls."

Evie hesitated, unsure, and then continued.

"Don't break those balls!" Beryl yelled again, with force. He turned and conferred with the men around him while Evie stood waiting.

"What are they playing for?" she heard a young man to her left ask another.

"Five-thousand," the other answered.

She looked at Evie who was talking with one of the men he came in with. She tried to make out what he was saying. "I haven't ever played a game of pool like this," she heard him say. His eyes were moist. He's afraid, Bernie thought.

"Okay, Evie," Beryl yelled. "We got the bets down. Go ahead and break 'em."

Red came over to her while Evie broke the balls. "We're in control now," he said, smiling. He won the next six games to take the lead.

Red kept an eye on Bernie while he played. She seemed comfortable enough being in the all-male environment and he was relieved. That afternoon, he had explained to her how Nine-Ball was played in hopes of making it more enjoyable for her. She had remained reserved for most of the game, but was beginning to show some signs of interest since he took the lead. He could see a little excitement in her eyes.

It was hard to keep his attention on his game, with her there, and it was costing him. He should have been two or three games ahead by now. He should be able to win twenty-one to eighteen, maybe even seventeen. As it was, he was at twelve, leading by one.

The next game, Red broke and took it all the way to the nine with an easy shot straight down the rail. He got down and stroked the cue ball three times. In the instant of execution, he thought of Bernie watching. It happened so quick, he was unable to stop himself. The nine hit the rail too full and jawed in the corner pocket—an easy out for Evie.

It was a lucky break for Evie and gave him a big dose of confidence. He ran two racks in a row and then played safe. Red kicked at the ball and missed by a hair. Ball in hand for the foul, Evie ran out again. The score stood at fourteen-twelve—Evie's favor.

Red took the next game and the one after that. "Good shot," Bernie said, as he walked past her to the end of the table. He smiled, then grimaced. He had momentarily forgotten her. He moved quick to break the balls, trying to stay ahead of the distracting thoughts he knew were coming. In his hurry, he hit the cue ball slightly off-center and it deflected to the left. By the time it hit the rack, it was a half-ball off of head-on. Half of the energy went into the rack and the rest stayed with the cue ball as it flew around the table—loose and dangerous. It was a weak break and nothing went in.

Evie ran three games in a row before Red got back on the table. They played a series of defensive games from there until the score stood twenty to nineteen in Evie's favor. Red was getting nervous—he had financially stretched both himself and Beryl to cover the match and side action. He didn't want to lose and he didn't like it that he had put himself in a pressure situation. Damn, he had wanted to impress Bernie with a big win.

Two men came in the front door and walked over to watch the game. One was a tall man with a balding head and hawk like nose. Red nodded at him. He was Mel Zedec, one of the big time gamblers in Detroit. He was a long-boned man—all arms and legs, with his legs from the knee down badly bowed. He looked as if he had grown too fast as a child, Red thought, with all the energy going into length. Zedec nodded back.

Red always made sure he was on his toes when Zedec was around. He was a excellent player and a dangerous adversary, with powerful and wealthy friends. Red looked to make sure Beryl had taken note of the newcomers. When Beryl nodded back, Red returned his attention to the game.

A few minutes later, Evie missed an easy shot on the six and Red jumped to his feet with excitement. The cue ball had rolled behind the seven-ball and stopped, blocking Red from seeing the six hanging on the lip of the corner pocket. Without hesitation, he banked the cue ball off the side rail. It rolled to the six and tapped it in. There

was a murmur of approval from the crowd—he could hear
Bernie among them. He turned and looked at her. He gave
her a big shit-eatin' grin, turned back to the table, and
fired in the seven, eight, and nine. The score was tied
twenty to twenty in a race to twenty-one—and Red had
the break.

"Red," Evie said. "You want to start over?"

"Start over? What the hell do I want to start over for?"

"We're tied with one game to go." Evie said. "That's
not a contest of skill. A man can win just by getting lucky
and shittin' the nine in. Let's start over and make a
challenge out of it."

"You want a challenge?" Red said, "I'll give you a
challenge—I'll *raise* you five-thousand!" He heard Bernie
gasp and he smiled. He knew what he was doing and so
did Evie. It was Red's break and if anyone was gonna shit
the nine in, it was two to one in his favor. There was no
more possibility of Evie taking a jack on the bet than there
was of Red starting over.

A disgruntled Evie racked the balls and sat down. Red
broke and the five went in the side. He chalked up and
looked to see where the nine-ball was. It hadn't moved at
all. He made the one and the two and left himself with a
long rail shot on the three. He paused to rethink his
strategy. The four was sitting in the middle of the short
rail and there was no easy way to get to it from the three.
He decided to shoot the three hard and hope the cue ball
would come off the three and hit the nine. If he got lucky
and the nine went in, he would win. If it didn't, he could

still play safe on the four. He got down, stroked the cue a couple of times, and let it rip. He followed the cue ball with his eyes after it hit the three. It went to the rail—hard—and left the surface of the table as it bulleted back. It was still in the air when it slammed into the nine. The nine took a beeline *right into* the far corner and the cue ball bounced its way to the opposite rail—bounced one final time—and landed *on the rail.* Red held his breath. The ball hesitated for a second, before rolling back onto the table and *directly* toward the other corner pocket. It was impossible to judge whether it would make it there or not.

"It's a scratch," he heard someone behind him say.

"Get in there!" Evie yelled.

The ball slowed as it rolled to the lip of the pocket. Red dropped the butt of his cue stick to the floor in a gesture of acceptance—and it *stopped*!

"Don't anybody move!" Beryl yelled. He counted out loud, "one-thousand—two-thousand—three-thousand—four-thousand—five-thousand. It's good!"

"Oh, my god," Bernie said.

Red twisted his cue apart and laid both halves on the table. He walked to the cue ball, put his index finger out, and barely touched it. It moved a thousandth of an inch and fell into the pocket.

Late the next morning, Bernie was sitting on the bed, still in her nightgown, with both legs tucked underneath. In front of her on the bed was all the money Red had won the night before. The bills were spread out randomly and covered the entire bed. She couldn't believe it. It didn't seem real.

She gathered up the money and rearranged it in neat rows according to denomination. There were tens, twenties, fifties, and hundreds. Never in her life had she seen so much money.

"I can't believe this is all ours," she said when Red came in from the kitchen. He was freshly showered and wearing a hundred-dollar shirt with cuff links, a pair of four-hundred dollar shoes, and bib overalls.

He sat on the bed. "Why don't you go and spend some of it today. You can drop me off at the Rack and go to the mall or something."

"Okay."

Red counted out two-thousand dollars into separate piles of two-hundred each. He rolled each pile into a tight roll and put a rubber band around it. "These are what players call *bundles*, or *balls*. Sometimes they call 'em *bullets*. If you ever hear someone ask 'how many bullets you got in your gun', this is what they're talkin' about. How many games can you lose without going bust." He put five of the balls in his left pocket and five in his right. "Let's go," he said.

Bernie dropped him off and drove a couple of miles to Northland Mall. She had a thousand dollars cash in her purse and held it with a tight grasp as she walked through the mall—stopping from time to time to look in the shop windows. She wished she would have brought Janet or someone else with her. She felt nervous and giddy.

She sat on a bench in front of Hudson's and smoked a cigarette. When it was down to the filter, she crushed it out, got up, and went into the store. She looked at several different items before selecting a white cashmere sweater with pearls sewn along the neckline and down the sleeves. It cost seventy-five dollars.

After the clerk rang it up, Bernie fished a hundred-dollar bill from her purse and held it out. The girl took it, gave her change, and wrapped the sweater with tissue paper and put it in a fancy box. When she held the box out to Bernie, the unreal became real—the unbelievable became believable.

"Wait a minute, honey," she said, "why don't you hold that box for a minute. I've got a few other things I want to get."

17

MILLIONAIRES

Frank Bryce made his millions just like Kilroy predicted. One day he came in the Rack with one arm wrapped around an A & P shopping bag. "I have arrived!" he yelled in his big, booming voice. Everyone stopped what they were doing and watched as he walked to his favorite table. "Gentleman," he said, "the price of pool has gone up!" He emptied the contents of the shopping bag onto the table. "There's fifty-grand here. Who wants to take a shot at it?"

There was a rush of activity. Men huddled together in small groups to combine funds and create a game they thought could win. Frank, no dummy, turned down the first three offers. The pay phones along the back wall were crowded with guys waiting to use them. One of the outgoing calls reached Red. "You better get down here fast, man," the bird dog said.

When Red got there forty-five minutes later, the room was packed. Every big time gambler he knew was in the room, most of them standing around the pool table where Frank and another guy were playing. Mel Zedec and a couple of his honchos were off to one side. A big, black man with a four inch scar down his cheek was on the other side. He was called Bones—not for his build, which was thick and meaty—but for his fondness for dice. He was the most successful black gambler Red knew and was always accompanied by two or three young black toughs.

Gil and his new partner, Al Simon, were at the counter. Al was a tall, slender man in his late fifties. Dapper in an expensive, tailored suit and always trying to make people laugh, Al was a friend of Frank's and one of the "Millionaire Jews." He had made his money in Miami—in the restaurant business, gambling, and god knows what else. He was the slickest person Red had ever met, not counting Titanic Thompson. He knew the edge on just about everything, but, like Thompson, couldn't shoot a lick of pool. Red walked over.

"Hey, Gil—hello, Al. What's going on? Who's taking the money down?"

"That prick—Zedec," Al said.

"You sound like he's takin' some of yours."

"No, I just hate the fucker."

Red was silent.

"You a friend of his, Cornbread?"

"Not me."

"Good," Al said, reaching into his suit coat. "Why don't you take this thousand and go over and mess with his head?"

"He won't play me," Red said.

"He will if he knows it's my money. He hates me, too." Al laughed. "Give him a game and make him play, Red. Beat his ass."

"All right." Red shrugged his shoulders, took the thousand, and walked over to where Zedec was standing.

Mel wouldn't play. Period. He had all of Frank Bryce's side action and was doing his best to hang on to it. Bones, who recognized a good deal when he saw one, was trying to get it for himself. "Come on," he said to Frank, "he's only giving you six-to-five. I'll give you seven-to-five if you take ten grand of it."

Frank, already down twenty-some-thousand, laughed. "Let me shoot, Bones," he said. "Go get your own game. Play Cornbread or someone." He nodded in the general direction of Red, still standing with Zedec.

"You *can* be played, Bones," Red said.

"Maybe. But not by you."

Red walked around the end of the table and stopped a few inches from the black man's face. "What'd you want to do, Bones?"

"I wanna see you play him," he said, pointing to one of his young men. "Get some of your people together. See if you can get my ten G's covered."

Red went back and talked to Gil and Al. He watched as they discussed the opportunity with one of the other "Millionaire Jews," and then with Bones. He laughed when he realized it wasn't any different now than it was in Three-Way Billiards when he was thirteen—just bigger bags of money.

That was the day the Rack took off. In the next few months, it kept going and growing. Gil hired Kilroy to run the register and to keep everyone in line. Kilroy put a Beretta .25 in his back pocket and got to work. He called every high roller, gambler, scoundrel, and player he had met in ten years on the road. With the word out, players and gamblers from all over the country started making their way to Oak Park.

"Isn't it something?" Kilroy said to Red one day. "It just seems that money draws money. I talk to a guy on the phone and let him know we got some millionaires in here and the guy is in here within a week. Doesn't matter *where* he was when I called him."

More millionaires came. The Rack developed into the Mecca for pool players—the Hollywood of the aspiring. The incredible amount of money circulating there made it the number one stop for anyone trying to make a living shooting pool. It was a chance to hit the big time. Players who didn't have someone to vouch for them, to get in, did their best to meet someone who could and would. It wasn't unusual, on any given night, to have a hundred and fifty people inside gambling.

It was inevitable for different groups and cliques to form. Besides the handful of millionaires, there were no regulars who could put up the stakes required to get in the *big games*. Groups were required to pool resources, to lay bets down together, to work out scams, and to find the *edges*. These groups worked the out-of-towners and outsiders who came in to take a crack at the opportunity of playing pool for five and six-digit figures. Many of them were overeager and made bad games. In fact, most of the top players who came to town returned home without their bankrolls.

One of the groups was headed by Mel Zedec, another by Bones, and the third, which Red was affiliated with, by

Al Simon. When they weren't vying for the attentions of an out-of-towner, they were gambling head-to-head with each other. There were advantages and disadvantages to having partners. Red profited by having access to the financial power and accumulated wisdom of the group, but he suffered from bad decisions he was expected to go along with. A lot of the bad decisions came from Al. Red couldn't believe that someone so intelligent, and so crafty, could make such bad games when it came to pool. Al could see everybody else's games in proper perspective, but when he himself was playing, it was like he suddenly got stupid—making games he couldn't possibly win. When Al was in one of these *playing* sprees, as he called them, both of the other groups met him at the door— excited and eager to play. Every time he played, he dropped fifty-grand. If Red had a piece of Al's action, he always did something to back himself up—he'd get someone to secretly lay a few grand on Al's opponent.

For Al, who could easily cover his own action, having partners wasn't a requirement—it was part of the excitement, part of the drama. It was how he inflated his confidence in his own game. He didn't like to stand alone and would rather *give* a piece of the pie away than do so. Cornbread was one of his favorite partners.

It was hot one afternoon and the doors of the Rack were wide open. Al waved to Red from one of the back tables when he came in. Red walked over.

Al was playing a guy Cornbread had seen shooting at another Oak Park room last year. He had looked pretty good then and Red was positive Al would come up short on this one—probably badly so.

"Hey, Cornbread, my redheaded friend, you want to get in on some of this action?" Al's face was flushed. As usual, he was excited and happy to be in a game.

"I can't Al, I'm flat busted." His hand moved instinctively over his right pocket to conceal the lump showing from the tight roll of hundred-dollar bills inside.

Al walked up to him while the other guy was shooting. "I heard you and Bennie won a hundred-and-forty-thousand last week. Did you have a problem collecting?"

"Little bit."

"Do you need some help with it? I know Frank pretty good—I can get it settled for you."

"No," Red said calmly. "It got settled. We had two other guys in with us and after we paid twenty for the table, I only had thirty coming. I didn't get it until Tuesday and had to settle for twenty."

"Where's that?"

"I lost it playing One-Pocket yesterday."

Al noticed his opponent sitting in the chair and realized it was his shot. He walked back to the table and continued speaking as he chalked up. "Where's Bernie?"

"She went down south for a few days."

Al took a shot and stood back up. "Every time you win any money your wife goes to Kentucky. I believe it's true what they say."

"What's that?"

"Bernie takes all that money down south."

"I wish."

Al missed an easy bank that rolled safe. He was pleased with his good luck. "They say she keeps it all in a coffee can down there," he laughed. "She buries it in a graveyard." He laughed again. When he missed, he walked back to where Red was standing. "I'm giving you five percent even if you are broke. Say I'm doing it cause I like your wife." He laughed again.

Great, Red thought. He sat down against the wall in a chair about twenty feet away from Al's table. He wanted to be close to appease Al, but he was a lot more interested in a match going on a few tables away. A guy from Chicago was playing Nine-Ball for a hundred a game with one of the Rack regulars. They were playing *ten ahead*, which meant they would play until one man got ahead ten and won, and then they'd settle up.

A few minutes after Red sat down, the Chicago player took his shirt off, walked down the row of tables past the spectators, and laid it on an empty table. He came back to the table he was playing on and played for another hour before falling ten games behind. He walked back to his shirt, picked it up, and took out a roll of hundreds. He counted out ten of them, stuck the rest back in the pocket, and laid the shirt down. He walked past the spectators, gave the cash to his opponent, and offered to do it again.

"Man," Red said to Kilroy, who was walking by, "what kind of a joint you running here? A guy can leave all that money laying there and no one's gonna walk off with it?"

"Hey," Kilroy said. "Nothing but the best for you, Red." He paused to light up a Pall Mall. "They know I'm committed, Red. That I'm responsible for these people bringing money in here. I'm watching all the time, looking for a heist coming down. They got to play position for a heist, ya know. They got to find out who's packin' pistols. I see anybody playing position for a heist, I'm gonna pull the plug on 'em. Just like that. Instant death." He walked back toward the counter.

Red understood completely. The toughest guys in town would gladly fork over their cash if you beat them on the pool table, or outwitted them in a proposition bet, but any one of them would probably die before they'd let someone steal it. Interesting in light of what Gil had told him: that 85% of the big money coming through the Rack was ill-gotten—heist money, drug money, extortion money, even murder money. He didn't know if it was true, and he didn't really care. As long as he could get out with the money, it didn't matter where it came from. All that mattered was getting it, and that meant finding an edge.

He had learned from Titanic the importance of having an edge. You could take any variable and use it to your advantage. You just had to stay on your toes and keep your eyes open. If you knew something the other guy didn't know, then it could be used to win. He knew for instance, that Kilroy had a cue stick shaft drilled out and filled with lead—it weighed almost twelve ounces. He could shoot as well with it as he could with his full size cue. A sure winner if he could get a game with a big spot for shooting with just the shaft.

Another guy in the Rack had taken three house cues to a cue maker and had them machined to the exact specifications of his personal cue—the same weight, taper, tip, and balance. In the middle of making a game he'd say: "Come on—I'll play you with a cue right off the rack." If his opponent agreed, he'd make a big show of selecting a cue—picking up and discarding several, before choosing his own—completely nullifying the spot except in the other guy's mind. Red, without seeming too eager, would pick up as much side action as he could.

One of the best things he ever saw was Al Simon throwing a cigarette in the air to get it to stick in the cracks between the ceiling slats above the snack bar. He practiced with several different brands and techniques. He must have been at it for a couple of hours one night. The next day, as if on a whim, he bet some of Zedec's bunch that he could do it within three tries. The damn thing was *still* up there.

Red watched as the Chicago man went back to his shirt for another thousand. It was amazing how eager some of these guys were to give their money away. He had realized a long time ago that there were only two types of gamblers. One was out to get the money, and one was out to give it up. He had a philosophy about it. If a guy had money he "wasn't supposed" to have, he'd probably give it up when it came down to fighting for it. On the other hand, if the guy believed he deserved it, and really needed it, he would fight like the dickens to keep it.

It got to where Red would even ask a prospective opponent: "Can you afford to lose the money?" If the answer was 'no,' or if the guy was slick enough not to answer the question—Red would pass on the game. If the guy said 'yes,' Red would play. If the guy was like Frank Bryce, whom Red had actually seen throw six-hundred bucks in the air once just to see people scramble for it— well, that was the kind of guy he wanted to play. Hell, that's the kind of fool *he* was before he met Bernie.

Red looked around the poolroom one more time and decided to head home. Bernie was supposed to call from down south in an hour and he didn't want to miss her. He said good night to Al and left.

18

Blood and Money

The next time he saw Al, Red was at the Rack with Bernie. "Hey, Al, where's your Cadillac? I didn't see it in the parking lot."

"Ahhh, I had to park it a couple blocks away," he answered. "Kilroy came and picked me up."

"What the hell for?"

"My wife's giving me a hard time about gambling and I don't want her to know I'm here. I packed my bags this morning and told her I was going to Miami for a business meeting. But I'm not doing anything for the next three days except gamble and play pool." He looked at Bernie and grinned. "I don't say a thing about it when she spends fifteen-thousand on a rug or some other bullshit."

"Where are you staying?" she asked.

" I got a room over at the Michigan Inn."

"Hey," Red said. "How did you do with that Oak Park shooter?"

"Not too good, Red."

"You lose?"

"Yeah."

"What do I owe for my five percent?"

"Six-thousand."

"Six-thousand? Man, don't be giving me that five percent any more. Damn, Al, you got to talk to me before you make these games—geez." Red shook his head in disgust.

"You can pay me later," Al said. "We've got more important things to talk about now. Here, Bernie. Here's a couple hundred for you to bet with. Your friend Beryl's down at the other end, why don't you go and bet on him? I've got to talk to Red for a moment."

"Sure," Bernie said. She took the money and gave Red a kiss on the cheek. "I'll see you in a bit."

"What's up, Al?" Red asked as she walked away.

"Zedec's supposed to be bringing a big shot in here tonight. A real big shooter who likes to play. They've already beaten him out of a half-million playing craps. They say he'll bet a hundred-grand at a pop."

"What's his name?"

"Eddie Reuben. He owns a shipping company and a lot of other businesses. You wouldn't know it if you saw him, though, he looks like he doesn't have a nickel."

"Is he the one they call Rubie?" Red asked.

"That's him. A redheaded guy with a lot of gray in it. Always wearing mismatched clothes—polyester slacks and weird sweaters—things like that."

"What's the deal?"

"Zedec's bringing him here to play you. Says you can spot him big and win all night as long as you let him make a lot of balls."

"What's in it for Mel?"

"We give him a slice of the action and keep quiet about it. You got any problem with that?"

"Not at all."

A little later, Red was sitting with Bernie when Zedec came in with two regulars and a small Jewish man. He was dressed like Al said he would be—plaid pants that looked like they were bought at a discount store and a button-down shirt ten years out of style.

"This is Rubie," Zedec said to Cornbread. "He read about you in the paper once and wants to play. You interested?"

"Sure." They worked out the details. Red would spot Rubie the break, the seven, the eight, and the nine for a thousand a game. Zedec would referee.

"Where's the money?" Bernie asked when Red was several games ahead.

"Don't worry about it. We'll get paid."

They played for a couple of hours with Rubie giving it his best. Red let him make a lot of balls in the games he lost, and he let him win one out of every three games. When Red was seventeen games up, however, Rubie lost interest in the match.

"I'm tired of this, Mel," he said to Zedec, "let's go to the track." He put the house cue he was using back on the rack and wrote Red a check for seventeen-thousand. As they were leaving the room, Red overheard them talking. "You almost had him there, Rubie," Zedec said. "I thought you were gonna win for sure."

"I'll get him next time," Rubie replied.

Red was looking forward to that next time, but it didn't seem like it was meant to be. He missed Rubie the next two times he was in the Rack and when they were finally both there at the same time, Rubie was already playing another hustler. The same thing happened the next time, too. Red was missing out on the big action. Al was absent—on a real business trip this time—and Red wasn't able to get it going on his own. He made a game with one of Bone's people, but overreached and got his butt kicked. He sent a friend home to get some money from Bernie to try and recoup, but he lost that, too. When he got home that night, Bernie was furious.

"Don't you ever send someone here to ask me for money," she screamed, shaking her finger in his face. "I didn't even know him."

Red kept his cool. "All right, all right," he said, trying his best to calm her down. "I won't do it again. I promise. Never again."

The next night, he took her out to make up for it. They had dinner at a nice restaurant and went to a local bar afterwards for a couple of drinks. They ran into a man there who had gambled with Red years earlier at the Hole. He was fresh out of prison and looking to celebrate. He joined them at their table and bought round after round— both he and Red excited and telling stories about the old days. At last call, all three of them were smashed. Red suggested they get a bottle of whiskey and go to the Rack.

Bernie drove while Red bragged to the other man about the Rack. They killed a third of the bottle by the time they got there and found the parking lot full and cars up and down the side street. They parked two blocks away and took ten minutes to laugh and stagger their way to the front door. It was locked. Red banged on the plate-glass door with his right hand, his left still holding the whiskey bottle, now two-thirds empty.

Kilroy came to the door and looked through the glass at the three of them. He made a motion as if to unlock the door, but stopped when he saw Red hand the whiskey bottle to the other man. He opened the door, but only a crack. "What do you want, Red?"

"Open the door, goddammit," Red said, staggering.

"I don't think so, Cornbread. Go home and sleep it off. I'll see you tomorrow."

"Tomorrow? What the fuck you talkin' about. Open the door." He tried to push the door, but Kilroy had his foot against it.

"I mean it, Red. I've got two-hundred of the biggest high rollers in the state here, and *you're* drunk. I'm not letting you in." He pushed on the door to close it—Red resisting. "Go home, Red."

"Come on. Bill," Bernie said, pulling his sleeve, "let's go. We can come back tomorrow." Red jerked his arm away from her just as Kilroy pressed the door shut and turned the latch.

"Goddammit!" Red kicked the door with his foot— once—twice—three times. Kilroy turned and walked away. "Motherfucker!" Red slammed on the glass with both arms. "Open the fucking door!" He banged on the glass with each syllable— "Open—the—fuck—ing—"

The glass *burst* into pieces as Red's arms penetrated it—blood spraying in all directions.

"Oh, my god!" Bernie cried.

Red fell to his knees, still holding his arms out in front of him. He was stunned—overwhelmed. Blood was everywhere. For a moment, he didn't know where he was. He felt strangely removed—almost peaceful. "Tommie?" he heard a voice say. After what seemed like a long pause, he recognized it as his own. He was trying to figure out what it all meant when he heard Kilroy's gruff voice.

"Jesus Christ! Red! Settle down." He grabbed a handful of Red's shirt and pressed it tightly against his bleeding forearm. "Call an ambulance," he said to Bernie.

Red passed out in the ambulance. When he woke, he was in a narrow white bed with metal sides. "Where's Bernie," he asked the nurse at his side. He tried to sit up but was restrained by a belt around his chest.

"Please don't move around, sir," the nurse said. "Your wife will be here shortly—and look—here's the doctor." Red turned his head to see a dark-haired man leaning over to look at his arm.

"Am I all right, Doc?"

"You've severed an artery and a tendon as big around as a pencil. We need to operate immediately."

"No way," he said, trying to get up again. "No one touches me until Bernie gets here."

"We have to get to that tendon as soon as possible."

"This is a million-dollar arm," Red insisted. "No one touches it until Bernie gets here." A few minutes later, he passed out again.

19

MARRIED LIFE

"That's it," Bernie said when he got out of the hospital. "If you want to be with me, there's no more drinking. I mean it, Red. I'm not gonna live with that."

Red squirmed uncomfortably on the couch. His arm inside the cast itched ferociously and his body had the heeby-jeebies from being in bed for a week. "All right, Bernie," he said, "I don't need to drink. If you don't want me to, I won't."

He convalesced for seven weeks and was a sweetheart the entire time. He helped Bernie with the chores—setting the table, cooking breakfast, even vacuuming a couple times. One day he drove himself to a dermatologist's office to find out about having his tattoos removed. He told Bernie about it later. "They charge by the inch," he said, "and it's supposed to be painful. But if it'll make you happy, I'll do it."

"I'd rather spend the money on a house of our own, Bill."

"You want a house?"

"Yes."

"Where you want this house?"

"On the other side of Melvindale. One of those pretty little brick ones."

"Let's take a ride—show me."

Bernie took him to her favorite neighborhood. It was modest, clean, and well-groomed. There were flowers in front of the houses and late model cars in the driveways. She pointed out one house and they parked in front. For almost an hour, Bernie shared with him how she would decorate the inside—the curtains, the furniture, the knick-knacks. She described how she would landscape the front—the bushes, the flowers, the ramp for Greg's wheelchair. Red could see it in his mind as she spoke.

It became a project for the two of them. Red contacted "California" John, a player he knew who was now in real estate and John came over and showed them what to do to buy a house. Red's income could not be documented, so they would have to pay cash or go with a land contract—both ways requiring a sizable hunk of money. For the first time in his life, Red had something he wanted that required planning and saving. As soon as the doctor removed the cast, he got to work.

He ran into Rubie in a small poolroom on Telegraph Road and enticed him with a ridiculous spot—the break, six, seven, eight, and nine for two-fifty a game. They played for two hours, neither getting ahead. Red planned to hold back until Rubie believed he could win and then jump the bet as high as he could—ringing up as many wins as he could before the little man quit. He called for a break, went to the phone, and called Bernie. "Come on down here and hold the money for me," he said, "bring me some good luck."

Red understood the value of patience. When it was almost time for the room to close and it still didn't feel right to jack the bet, he resigned the day to being a set-up—a day spent playing with nothing to show for it, except a probable pay off in the future. Much to his surprise, the other man jumped the bet. "Here's my address, Cornbread. Bring all the money you got in thousand-dollar balls, and we can keep playing on my seven-footer. Bring your wife, if you want."

Red and Bernie stopped at home and made seven rolls of a thousand-dollars each. They got back in the car, Bernie driving, and followed Rubie's directions to his home in Taylor. It was a big, impressive looking house. "If he'll keep playing long enough," Red joked, "we could get a house like this for ourselves." Bernie laughed.

Rubie met them at the front door. "This is my wife's collection," he said as they walked through the formal living room. It was full of expensive antiques and sectioned off by a padded velvet rope strung between two brass stands. "Wow," Bernie said, "it looks like a museum."

They followed him down the stairs to the basement. There was a seven-foot pool table sitting in the middle of a shockingly dumpy room. The carpet was a light rose color, long-napped and cheap—loose and bunched up in the corners. Four or five cats lounged around the room— two on the sofa, others on the floor. A fluffy white one stood up, stretched itself with an arched back, and came over and rubbed against Bernie's leg. Rubie kicked it away.

"You like country music, Bernie?" he asked.

"Oh, I love it."

"Pick out anything you like here," he said. He pointed to a large entertainment center, complete with expensive stereo and shelves full of records. Bernie picked out a Loretta Lynn album and put it on. The sounds of "Coal Miner's Daughter" came out of four big speakers spread around the room. She walked over and took a chair by the end of the pool table where Red was standing.

The men played a few games and Cornbread won most of them. After every win, Rubie would toss a thousand-dollar *bundle* to Red and Red would toss it to Bernie. Once in a while, Red would lose and Bernie would toss a bundle to him and he would toss it back to Rubie. After Bernie accumulated about a dozen of these, she took them into the bathroom to steal a few hundred to hide from Red. When she broke open the first ball and counted it, there was only nine-hundred there. She took another ball out of her purse and removed the rubber band and counted—it too was a hundred short. She emptied the contents of her purse onto the vanity and separated all the balls from the other stuff. She inspected every ball—six of twelve were short. She went back to her chair by the pool table.

As soon as Red missed, she motioned him over. "Red," she whispered, "some of these bundles are short."

He held his hand up to stop her. "Don't even say a thing," he whispered back, "I'm gonna win us all the money we need right here." It was something he'd learned from Oakland Don—*never argue when you're ahead.*

When Rubie finally quit, the sun was coming up. Red and Bernie stopped at a restaurant and took seats in a half-circle booth in the rear. After they ordered breakfast, Bernie, in the back of the booth, carefully unwrapped each ball and stacked the bills just out of sight on the red vinyl seat. She looked up and acted natural when the waitress brought their coffee and returned to her counting when she left. When it was all counted, she took a sip of coffee and looked at Red with a smile. "We've got eighteen-thousand here," she said, "enough for a down payment."

They closed on a perfect house, a block down from the one they had parked in front of a month earlier. The first night there, with things still scattered about in boxes and bags, she agreed to marry him. They got married at the Candlelight Wedding Chapel in Vegas a few weeks later when one of the casinos hosted a tournament.

Red introduced her to Danny Jones, Fats, and a lot of the other players. They all congratulated them on their wedding and showed surprise when Red refused the offered drinks. Bernie was impressed to see how well received he was. Several of the players referred to him as *The Living Legend*. She had not realized either the extent of his fame or the number of his friends. She particularly liked Danny Jones. She liked how the tall, good-looking man whistled and sang when he played pool.

Red did poorly in the tournament—winning nothing and losing the entry fee. Bernie got upset, and accused him of not trying hard enough. Later, when he was in a gambling match, she groaned and yelled at him every time he missed. After he lost most of their money, Danny Jones pulled her aside. "You're being a little rough on Red," he said.

"We can't afford to lose that money," she defended. "We've got bills to pay—house payments and insurance and a lot of other things. He needs to win."

"Bernie," he said, in a patronizing tone. "He's not *going* out there to lose, for christsake. He's *trying* to win. Cut him some slack. He can't play good with you on his back."

Bernie was quiet for a moment.

"He'd do a lot better if you were on his side."

"Okay," she said, nodding her head, "I'll try to do better."

"That's a girl." He gave her a squeeze on the shoulder and turned to walk away.

"Wait a minute, Danny," she said, stopping him. "How come he never does any good in these tournaments?"

"He's not a tournament player."

"What do you mean?"

"There's two kinds of pool players—tournament players and gamblers. Red's a gambler—he plays his best when he's in a long match with just one guy. He beats 'em down and grinds 'em up. Tournament play is over too quick for Red's style."

Later, in their room, she apologized to Red. "I'm sorry I yelled at you," she said, "I know you were trying your best. I won't do it again."

"Don't worry about it," Red responded. "I'm gonna win it all back tomorrow on the craps table."

The next afternoon, Red went down to the casino with Billy Johnson, a player who was leading in all three divisions of the tournament and was a big favorite to win. They pooled their resources—a grand total of seventy dollars, and went to a five-dollar minimum craps table. Red played for both of them. He waited until someone he liked had the dice before laying a single chip on the pass line and another behind it for the odds. The shooter hit a seven and threw another four passes before crapping out. Red took the dice when offered to him and held on for another ten passes, betting all the way. When he passed the dice to the next shooter, they had over three-hundred dollars. "Let's start betting twenty-five-dollars a shot," he said.

Billy Johnson agreed and they continued until Red had a huge pile of red chips in front of him. When the dice were offered to him, Red stood up, stretched, and looked at the three other players and then the pit boss. "We'll trade all these red ones for hundred-dollar chips," he said. When they were exchanged, he sat back down with an excited Billy Johnson standing behind him. Before the dice were passed out, they were joined by another man, from the tournament, who remembered Red's incredible run at the Stardust a few years earlier. Two others took places, and then another. Within minutes, the table was full—every position taken. When the dice were handed to Red, every man bet the pass line. He threw eight passes in a row before surrendering them. The pit boss offered them to each shooter in turn, working his way around the table in clockwise fashion. All declined and the dice went back to Red. He threw pass after pass—oblivious to everything except the dice and the felt. When he finally crapped out, they were up to ninety-thousand.

"One more time!" Red said. "One more time!" He held on—still playing the odds and buying come numbers at a thousand dollars a piece. In ten minutes, after a third of their chips had disappeared, Billy Johnson pulled him from the table.

"That's it, Red," he said, his face shiny with perspiration. "It's time to quit, man. It's time to walk away."

Red nodded, his hands shaking. They gathered up the chips—red, black, white, and green. Surrounded by pool players, they walked into one of the lounge areas and commandeered a table. Red sat down and lit a cigarette— hands calmer, but still shaking. "Man, that was fantastic," he said.

They divided the chips up into piles of five-thousand and added it up. They had over fifty-six-thousand. Billy Johnson ran to the tournament room and got three more guys to go to the cash window for them. When it was all cashed out, they paid each man a hundred bucks and divided the rest—half for Johnson and half for Red.

"Let's go back in the tournament and pass a few of these hundreds around," Red said.

Billy Johnson begged off. "Not me," he said, "I'm too wired. I'll take care of those guys tomorrow. I'm gonna go to the gym and work these jitters off. I'll see you in the morning."

Red had a stack of hundreds an inch and a half thick. He took the elevator up to his room, opened the door, and threw the stack on the bed where Bernie was lying down, watching TV. "Get up and get dressed." he said. "We're going down to the tournament and spread some happiness around."

Bernie was elated. She showered and dressed before remembering the stories of Red's other big wins. "Don't even *think* about giving this money away," she said. "You're a married man now and you got bills and a family. We need this money."

Red agreed to limit what he passed around. "But I gotta give at least a fifty or a hundred to some of these guys," he said. "They're the guys who'll flip me a hundred when I'm down. I gotta do the same when I'm up."

They left the room and took the elevator to the first floor. The doors opened to a lobby crowded with people going different ways. They got out of the elevator and headed toward the tournament room. In a flash, Red saw Evie about twenty feet away. Without thinking, he yelled at him. "Evie! Come on, sucker. I'll play you for twenty G's. Right now!" He threw the stack of money across the room to Evie. Evie saw it coming and threw up both hands in an attempt to catch it, but the throw was too wide. It clipped the edge of one hand, ricocheted to the right, and came apart in the air.

"No!" Bernie yelled as bills exploded into the crowd.

"Don't no one kneel!" Red shouted. He dropped to the floor with Evie and Bernie—frantically gathering loose bills together and pushing people away. Bernie filled both hands and stuffed it in her purse. Red stuffed both pockets of his sport coat and did his best to hold more with an arm pressed to his chest. As soon as the area was contained with the help of two casino employees, Red started an orderly stack.

"We only lost two hundred," he said to Bernie, after he stopped in the men's room for a count. They continued to the tournament room where Red passed out what he thought was necessary and then they went shopping. Red took her to the same shop he had taken the others to a few years earlier. They picked out complete wardrobes and had them delivered to their room. They stopped back at the tournament and gambled for another hour before returning to the room themselves.

The next morning, they prepared for the flight back to Detroit. Red left Bernie to do the packing while he went to meet Danny Jones for breakfast. He was carrying the money on him. He sat in the lobby, just outside the restaurant on one side and the corridor to the casino on the other. He could hear the slot machines and the other casino noise—still going strong at eight in the morning. He waited for Danny until eight-fifteen, and then went to the counter. "I'm waiting for a tall guy with dark hair. If he shows up here, tell him I stopped at the crap tables for a quick one." The clerk agreed.

A half an hour later, Bernie was still packing and expecting Red back at any moment. Their flight was at ten-forty-five and they had planned to leave by ten. There was a knock at the door.

"Bernie!" she heard Red yell. "Open the door!"

She turned the latch and Red came in. She could tell right away that something was wrong. "What's the matter, honey?" she asked.

"I lost it," Red said without looking at her.

"You lost what?"

"I lost the whole *fucking* thing!" he yelled. He threw his keys at the TV. They bounced off the screen with a loud, metallic clank.

"What do you mean you lost the *whole* thing?"

"Just like I said, goddammit! I lost the whole *fucking* twenty-thousand!" He knocked the open suitcase off the bed—spilling the new clothes across the room and on the floor. He went into a fit of rage, kicking and swearing. He yanked the doorwall open and grabbed a handful of clothes.

"I don't want any of this shit!" he screamed. He threw them over the balcony railing and grabbed another armful.

"I want mine!" Bernie screamed back at him. She grabbed his arm and tried to pull him away from the clothing. Both of them fell to the floor—yelling and screaming.

20

COMING APART

It was unusual for Red to blow up around Bernie. He was usually low-key and easy going around the house, and if he needed to vent—to get loud and expressive, he took it to the Rack. There, he was in his element and was expected to be brash and foulmouthed.

In the months following their return from Vegas, he turned more and more of the control of the money over to Bernie's hands. When flush, he would keep a part of the cash to gamble with and give the rest to her. When he was down and needed a stake, she would dole it out in little pieces; sometimes only enough for smokes and lunch. Red didn't like asking her for money and would exhaust every possible source of funds before doing so. She was the bank of last resort.

Once, Bernie was at home when she received a phone call from a friend at the Rack. "You better get down here," he said. "Cornbread's shooting blindfolded for a thousand-dollars a game."

"A thousand-dollars? Blindfolded? Has he been drinking?"

"I don't think so."

She threw her purse in the car and rushed to the Rack. There, she rang the buzzer and was admitted. Red was at a table in the middle of the room surrounded by a throng of spectators. She watched as he considered his next shot and was relieved to see that he didn't have a white cloth around his eyes as she had imagined. After a second, he got down and positioned his body over the ball. He took careful aim, closed his eyes, and turned his head to the side. He shot. The object ball rolled to the far corner and missed by a good three inches. When he stood up and moved away from the table, Bernie walked over and tapped him on the shoulder.

"Do you know what you're doing?" she asked.

"Don't worry about a thing, baby. I'm already up thirteen-thousand."

She watched for a few more minutes and then went home.

The action continued on a big scale. As the fame of the Rack grew, so did the inexhaustible appetite of the resident gamblers. One hustler brought a seven-foot table in to play Rubie, who preferred that size. Others hounded Gil to allow other forms of gambling. He resisted for a long time before finally allowing Al Simon to run a table-less crap game in the card room. It competed with the full table crap game housed in the steam room across the street. The steam room was frequented by the "Millionaire Jews," who would sit in the steam bath until the sweat rolled down their big bellies, before getting rub downs from the German masseuses. Then they would relax over inch-thick steaks in the small dining room until the craps game started.

One day, a friend of Red's backed him in a One-Pocket game against Mike, a champion pool player from Miami. They played a thousand a game on the big ten-footer and generated a lot of interest and suspense. When Mike and his contingent of backers finally quit, Red and his friend were up ten-thousand and flushed with victory. They strutted around the poolroom and challenged everyone in the place to take a crack at the ten-grand. When nobody would, Red's friend suggested they go across the street and get in the crap game.

When they returned to the Rack an hour later, they were fifty-thousand richer and preceded by the news of their good fortune. Three different guys offered them games as soon as they came in the door. One guy, a friend of Zedec's, agreed to back Mike against Red for a thousand a game. Before it got going, Red and his friend took down another nineteen-thousand on the side.

Unbelievably, Red lost three games in a row—the entire sixty-thousand. He was furious with himself, but maintained an outer composure as he negotiated the backing for one more game. While the balls were being racked, he went to the cigarette machine for a pack of smokes. He put the change in and pulled the knob for Parliaments. Nothing came out. He hit the coin return to get his money back. Nothing happened. He pulled the knob again, and then hit the return—harder—then harder still. Again, nothing happened.

Red stood and looked at the face reflected in the glass of the cigarette machine. He used to be able to do this when he was younger, he thought. Lose big, piss it away, and never be concerned. He could always win it back tomorrow. He hit the coin return again as he realized those days were gone.

"Damn it!" he screamed, when the coins were still withheld. He grabbed the light-brown metal sides of the machine with both hands and shook it in convulsive anger.

No cigarettes. No change. Red stepped back from the machine and looked again at his reflection. He looked old. He became aware of the quiet and turned around to see everyone in the room looking at him.

"What the fuck you looking at?" he challenged. He walked back to the pool table and took his seat as Mike broke the balls. A few moments later, it was final—Red had lost eighty-thousand.

The constant stream of people and money coming through the Rack continued. Even to Red, who had seen plenty of high stakes pool in his day, it was astounding. One champion came in from the east coast with two backers and a suitcase filled with packets of money—each one bound by a narrow paper wrapping. A few days later, they returned to New York with an empty suitcase. Another player came in alone from Washington with two paper sacks full of loose bills. He stayed for a week and went back to the capital with an extra sack. The action was so good, and so steady, that many succumbed to it like a drug addict to an overabundance of drugs. The only thrill left to chase, the only mountain left to climb, was the one of excess. How high could you build it before it came tumbling down? Who could play for the largest amounts? Who could take the pressure? Al Simon was one of the ones who overdosed.

One day in November, he played One-Pocket with "California" John for five-hundred a game. John, financed by Red and two others, spotted Al eight-to-six and played one-handed to boot. After Red and his friends lost twenty-five-hundred of their three-thousand dollar bank, they quit, and the game died for lack of funding. They were trying to negotiate better terms, when Kilroy arrived.

He was wearing a gray skull cap with a hole in it. A button pinned next to the hole read: *My job is so secret, even I don't know what I'm doing.* A cigarette was stuck to the bottom of his upper lip. "Look here," he said, holding up a blank envelope, "I got the title to my car in here." He waved it at Al Simon, now sitting in a chair with cue stick in hand. "You want to play me for it, Al?"

"Is that the title for that junker you been driving?"

"That's a good car and you know it."

There were laughs of derision from several men. Kilroy ignored them. "I'll play you one-handed."

Al looked at him for a moment before replying. "I'll play, but if I win, I'm gonna burn that old, raggedy car."

They started playing. Red went together with John and another guy to bet against Al, who took all their action and that of three other groups. It started out light, but became serious as the day progressed. By the early evening, Al was two-hundred-thousand in the hole, with Red and his partners winning thirty-five of it. He paid off eight-thousand and promised to be back on Monday with the rest. It was common for the big shooters to run tabs. They were on the honor system—sometimes even paying by check. Rubie had started it when he wrote a company check to one of Zedec's cronies for a hundred-and-thirty-thousand. Since then, the practice had become popular. The winner had to get someone to cash it for him—always at a discount—and usually by someone who was *with* the guy who lost it. It was a way for the high rollers to minimize their loses.

A few days later, Kilroy said he wanted to talk. Red went with him in his raggedy car to the Nine Mile Deli where they got a table and ordered coffee and sandwiches.

"What's the matter with your voice?" Kilroy asked.

"I don't know," Red said, his voice scratchy. "Its been like this for a couple of days."

"You better go let a doctor look at that."

"Yeah, yeah. That's what Bernie said. I just got a frog in there." He paused as the waitress set the cups of coffee in front of them. "What's this you want to talk about?"

"A heist."

"What do ya mean a heist?"

"What I mean is when the wolves don't got nothing to eat, they start to eat each other. They start fingering the people with the money, with the bankrolls."

"No one's gonna heist the Rack," Red said. "Everybody knows everybody. They'd have to kill everyone in the place to get away with it."

"There's some strangers coming around—coming in with a friend of Al Simon's. I don't like them and I don't like the way they look. Guys who are okay don't even know who they are."

"Why don't you just bar them?"

"Come on, Red, I never barred a guy in my life. Even when they've come at me with knives and guns. You know that guy you were with when you broke the window? He's a pretty tough guy. One of those guys that—" his voice trailed off as the waitress returned with their sandwiches.

"Why don't you just tell Al, let him worry about it."

"His friend is a stone junkie. He's got no respect and he thinks he's smart by conning people, but he gets carried away. He's a stone junkie who's got nothing. He's a liar and a thief and a cheater." He took a bite of his corned beef. "Now he's bringing in guys from the penitentiary and shit that knows him. *Piasans* and all that bullshit."

"What are you gonna do?"

"I'm gonna take care of it. You can't go around heisting people without knowing who you're heisting." He took another bite and washed it down with a slug of coffee. "I still get around pretty good."

Two nights later it was cold and raining and a lot of the regular crowd stayed away. Kilroy pulled three-hundred dollars from the register and went around the room trying to get something going—to get the action stirred up—get the blood moving—get guys to the phones. That was the way the gambling scene worked. If a guy called in, he'd want to know what was going on. If nothing was happening, he'd call somewhere else. On the other hand, if something did get cooking, guys who were present called their friends to come and get in on it. Kilroy was flashing the three-hundred to Red and several others at the snack bar, when a siren went off in the parking lot. He ran to the door, closely followed by the others.

When he opened the door, there was a man standing there and another a few feet behind him. There was an official looking car—green—with an aerial in the center, sitting in the middle of the parking lot. The man in front had a fedora pulled low over his eyes and tilted to the side so the rainwater rolled off the brim and missed his face. Both of them wore trench coats.

"An alarm went off here," the one in front said.

"Thank you officer. Thank you very much," Kilroy replied. Red watched as the two men turned, walked to the green car, got in, and drove away. Kilroy pushed the door shut.

"Who the hell was that?" Red asked, his voice raspy and almost inaudible.

"Just a couple of cops. Hey, Harry," he yelled to a gambler still sitting at the counter. "Your alarm went off. You better go and check it out." He turned back to Red. "Man, you got to have a doctor look at your voice."

Red grunted and went back to the counter.

The next morning Red woke up and came to the kitchen for a cup of coffee. When he came around the end of the knick-knack wall that separated the hall from the kitchen, he was surprised to see Bernie sitting at the table with another man. It was Frank, a neighbor and friend from down the block. Red tried to say good morning to the big man, but no words came from his mouth.

"Sit down," Bernie said.

He sat down and tried to speak again. "What's going on?" He rasped, barely loud enough to be heard.

"You've got a doctor's appointment in forty-five minutes and you're going whether you want to or not. If we have to, Frank's gonna pick you up and put you in the car."

Red looked at Frank. He remembered when the refrigerator broke and they needed to bring the old one up from the basement. Frank had carried it up on his back—by himself. Red had held the basement door for him. "Okay," he whispered.

The three of them got in the Buick and drove to the hospital. After a short wait, Red was escorted into an examination room, where a doctor squeezed and poked. He put three different instruments down Red's throat before sending him to another room for X-Rays. Much to his surprise, they also took X-Rays of his chest. He was taken back to the first room he laid on the examination table and thumbed through a four month old news magazine. He was just finishing a story on race-fixing in New York, when Bernie came in and took a seat on the doctor's stool. Red sat up.

"What?" he croaked.

"They say you got cancer, Bill," she said, the fear showing in her voice.

Red followed the magazine with his eyes as he set it down. He steeled himself for a moment and then looked back at her. "How bad?"

"They won't know until they operate."

"What about my lungs?" He asked, remembering the X-Rays.

"They want to do a biopsy to be sure. There's something there, but they don't think it's cancer. The doctor asked me if you ever worked in the coal mines. Said there were specks on your lungs like coal miners get. I told him no."

"What do they think it is?"

"The doctor thought it might be pool chalk from shooting pool. He said maybe you've breathed a lot of it in."

On the morning of his surgery, he was given a shot of Demerol and shaved by a nurse. By the time two aides picked him up and put him on a cart, he was peaceful and relaxed. They moved into the hall, one pushing Red and one pulling the IV stand. Bernie walked on one side, holding his hand and speaking gently to him. When they got to the double doors of the operating room, the aides pushed him over to the wall and told him he'd be there for a few minutes. They disappeared through the double doors and he and Bernie were alone.

He motioned to Bernie, and she bent over to listen. "I always thought I'd get my throat cut one day," he whispered. He grinned when she pulled her head away to look at him.

"Don't fool like that," she said. "You're gonna be fine."

"I mean it," he said. "I found a man when I was a boy. Dick Stennen cut his throat 'cause he lost and didn't pay. I saw it, but I can't remember."

Bernie started to speak, but was interrupted by the opening of the doors and the return of the aides. She gave Red's hand one last squeeze as he was wheeled away.

21

BUSTED AGAIN

As soon as Red could speak, he called the Rack from his hospital bed. "What's going on?" he asked, when Kilroy answered the phone.

"I'm the only one here. I'm trying to get in stroke with nobody knowing about it. How are you feeling, Cornbread?"

"I'm all right. I gotta quit smoking and take some of those radiation things."

"Maybe you can chew tobacco when you get better."

"Maybe. Hey, what time is it?"

"About eight in the morning."

"Wow."

"You hear what happened?" Kilroy asked.

"No, what?"

Kilroy mentioned two gamblers who were regulars. "They got heisted."

"You're kidding!"

"No. They were walking to their cars a couple of nights ago. Three guys did it—two whites and a black. I know who they are, too—they're the same guys that were here that night the alarm went off—posing as cops."

"Those weren't cops?"

"Fuck no. They were busting into Harry's car—looking for the money. I didn't figure it out until the next morning when one of the neighbors brought over an insurance book he found in the parking lot. It was from another guy's Lincoln—same color as Harry's. They knew what they were looking for, but they broke into the wrong car."

"Who are they?"

"They came out of Jackson pen. They were champion fighters there—real tough guys. They ain't gonna last thirty days on the street after this."

"Do you know who brought them around?"

"I do. I told Gil about him. I said—'He's got to go, Gil.' He said—'he's a friend of Al Simon's.' I said—'I don't care—either he goes, or I do.' Gil told Al and he took care of it."

A nurse carrying a thermometer and a blood pressure gage came into Red's room. "I got to go," he said, "my nurse is here."

"See you later, Red."

"All right."

When Red made it to the Rack two weeks later, he could tell the difference right away. There was a dent in the armor—a breach in the imaginary wall that separated the Rack from the rest of the world. There had been a violation—the heist—and some of the magic had died. The big money people were the source of the magic, and they only showed up where their safety was guaranteed. No one said anything about it, but there were a few faces missing, and the ones who were still there, weren't flashing it around like they once did.

Frank Bryce still came in. So did Al Simon, Rubie, and a half dozen other high rollers. Mel Zedec was there almost every night—playing throughout the night and stopping immediately at seven in the morning for some mysterious reason of his own. Players from around the country still came, but not as many and not as often.

In the next few months, Red played every chance he got. He brought home an average of a grand a week and laid it on the kitchen table for Bernie, who no longer came with him. He tried to ignore the signs of decline that came to his attention. The trash that didn't get emptied and overflowed to the floor. The faucet in the bathroom that developed a leak and didn't get fixed. The weeds by the front door that took root in a parking lot crack and grew two feet high.

The tension that had always existed between some of the regulars escalated. There were arguments and fights. Al found out that Gil was sneaking around and betting against him when he played. To retaliate, he started stealing money out of the till. One day Gil caught him and it was the end of the partnership. They decided Al would pick a price and give it to Gil, and he, in return, could accept or reject it. He could pay Al the amount and own the place by himself, or he could take the money from Al and walk away.

"I'll give you thirty-five-thousand," Al said.

"No," Gil said. "I'll give *you* thirty-five-thousand."

A few days later, Gil fired Kilroy.

"What happened?" Red asked.

"He got mad because there wasn't any change in the register." Kilroy said. "I took it to get the action going. He doesn't understand how it works."

"Maybe you oughta put it back when you can."

"I did. When he came in yesterday, the three-hundred dollars he gave me for change was still there. He was mad because it was three one-hundred dollar bills."

"What are you gonna do?"

"I'm gonna go down to Tampa and visit a friend of mine."

"What do you think is gonna happen here?"

"I don't know, Red. The city inspectors came through last week and gave Gil about fifty code violations. I don't know, I really don't."

Red walked a few feet to the closest waste can. He pushed the hinged lid back with one hand, leaned close, and spit a stream of brown tobacco juice through the opening.

"Nice shot," Kilroy said. Both of them laughed.

After Kilroy left, the conditions at the Rack declined even further. A lot of the big time action shifted from pool to craps. Different customers started coming in, too. Most of them associated with Mel Zedec. Red just kept his eyes open and played whatever game the people with the money were playing.

Gil was sick. He complained about a spinal problem and was sometimes absent for days at a time. The deadline on the city code violations came and went without any corrections being made. The city inspected again, and in spite, slapped him with an additional twelve violations.

Red did his best to keep track of the rumors. He had the same degree of interest that a factory worker at Ford's would have regarding the health of the factory. He was used to the place and wished it the best, but he had no intention of going down with the ship. It was a developing drama and he did his best to walk the fine line between spectator and participant.

He was surprised one day to see Kilroy behind the counter. "What the hell are you doing here?" he asked.

"Gil called me down in Florida and asked me to come back."

"What for?"

Kilroy looked around to see if anyone else was listening. He motioned Red closer. "They're trying to shake Gil down."

"Who?" Red asked in alarm.

"Rat-Face Eddie and that stinkin' bunch. Trying to take our joint over—and Mel and the rest of those bums wouldn't even intervene to help. Gil called me to come in and straighten it out."

"What are you going to do?"

"I told Zedec—you got five days to straighten this out. Five days and then I'm gonna take care of it. I'll take care of every one of them."

"You better be careful."

"I don't care about it, Red. Zedec and all those other motherfuckers ran like dogs. Ran with their tails behind their ass—everyone scared to death. I don't give a shit. They got five days to straighten this out and if they don't, I will. I'll straighten it out where they won't *ever* forget about it. Never."

Red kept a low profile the rest of the week. He went to the Rack only in the daytime—even then cruising past the parking lot and checking out the cars before going inside. He didn't go in at night until he saw Al Simon's car outside. Al always knew what was going on before any one else did. If he was there, then the thing was settled.

Gil's health worsened. He was admitted to the hospital and an operation was performed to fuse his spine. It was several weeks before he was back at the Rack, moving around as little as possible and with great care when required to do so. He answered the phone one evening when Red called.

"What's going on?" Red asked.

"Zedec brought Rubie in. Bennie's got him on the seven-footer. You probably want to be in here."

"See ya in a few." Red said, hanging up the phone. He yelled to Bernie who was cooking dinner. "Throw something together for me to take, baby—Rubie's playing and I don't want to miss it." He hustled into the bathroom and lathered his face to shave. One of the good things about the forty-some radiation treatments was that he didn't have to shave under his chin anymore. He rinsed the excess lather off his hand and picked up his razor. This could be a good night, he hoped, remembering the last few days. He had waited around the Rack for three days for a big game that was supposed to happen. Finally, he couldn't stay awake any longer and went home to sleep. He found out later that as soon as he left, the guy with the money showed up and *went off* big time. He figured he probably lost fifteen-grand by going home. This could be the chance to make it up. He finished shaving, grabbed a sandwich from Bernie, and headed to the Rack.

When he got there, Rubie was playing a friend of Bones' on the seven-footer. Red got in with a bunch of men, including Bones, who were betting against the short Jew. They were playing Nine-Ball for five-thousand a game, with the black player spotting Rubie the six. Mel Zedec was doing the organizing. He had everybody's amounts written down on a piece of paper and changed the figures after every game. Every time the hustler shot, the room was quiet to allow him to concentrate. Every time Rubie shot, they yelled and jeered. They dropped things on the floor and shouted across the room—anything to distract him. He did his best to ignore them.

At one point, Rubie bent down to take an especially delicate shot on the nine. As he stroked the ball to find his aim, Bones yelled at him. "Ahhh—you can't shoot—ya bum." He took his final stroke, and missed. He threw the cue stick on the table and snapped in anger at the men. All of them burst into laughter. Red was still laughing as the john door closed behind him. He went into the single stall and sat on the commode. He was thinking about stopping in the card room to check on the crap game, when he was interrupted by two young black men coming in from the poolroom. They were talking loudly. Red looked through the crack between the door and wall and saw that both were sporting the new look of the eighties—rasta hair, matted and tangled. One had hair that was either dyed, or sun faded, a light reddish color.

"Bones ain't gonna give up no money," he said.

"That's right," the other one said. "We black brothers know how to take that money down."

Red smiled, thinking about all the money he had won from Bones over the years. If you only knew, he said silently to the young men. Just then, there was a terrible crashing sound from inside the poolroom. Red sat straight up—fully alert.

"What the fuck?" one of the black men said. They rushed to the door and yanked it open. Red could hear shouting and other loud noises as they left the room. One of the voices was amplified and Red knew immediately what was going on. He got to his feet, walked to the sink, and calmly washed his face. The din coming from the poolroom was tremendous. He dried his hands and face with a piece of paper towel and pulled the door open.

As soon as he stepped into the room, he was grabbed by a man in blue. Like forty or fifty others in the room, he was wearing a baseball cap with the letters FBI on the front. Red caught a glimpse of the bullet proof vest on the man's chest as he was spun around and pushed up against the wall. He was quickly and expertly frisked and led to the center of the room where Zedec, Bones, and the others were cordoned by a ring of baseball caps. Al Simon and another group of people were led in from the card room and pushed into the circle of captives.

"All right," said an official looking man with a bull horn. He was the only one without a baseball cap and not holding a weapon. Red could see a revolver handle sticking out of a small, brown holster under his left armpit. "Who's got the dice?" he bellowed over the bull horn. No one answered.

"We know you were playing craps in here. We want the dice. Who's got the dice?" He paused for a response that did not come.

"Search them again," he said to the officer standing next to him. The officer motioned to several others and the whole group moved into position and frisked the gamblers one after another. No dice were found.

"Find the dice," the leader said to the officer again. "Take the place apart if you have to."

For two hours, they turned over chairs, emptied the waste baskets, and looked in the obvious corners and crannies. They took the plumbing apart in both the john and snack bar. Much to the disappointment of the man with the bull horn, they did not find any dice. They picked up the horned battering ram they had used to smash the doors open and left.

The men in the poolroom milled about in relief— lighting cigarettes and joking with each other. In the next few minutes, many of them left and the ones remaining congregated at the snack counter. Two of them, at Gil's direction, passed out coffee and donuts.

"You guys want to see something funny?" Al Simon asked.

When he was answered by several voices of encouragement, he pulled a pack of Marlboros from the inside pocket of his expensive, tailored jacket. He tilted the pack and spanned it in front of the others so they could see the open top. It was a full pack—missing only one or two cigarettes. In dramatic fashion, he pulled one brown filtered end from the pack and dropped it to the floor. It was broken off a half-inch from the filter. He pulled two other broken ones out and dropped them to the floor. He looked around at the men.

"I'll bet you guys a thousand dollars I got a pair of dice in here."

Several of the men laughed. "No way," one of them said. Others agreed with him. Zedec pulled out a piece of paper and wrote down names and numbers as the men placed bets. When he was done, everybody looked back at Al.

He turned the pack of Marlboros over and gave them a shake. Nothing came out. He tapped the edge of the pack and shook them again. Two red dice fell into his hand.

22

RESOLUTION

The pressures on Gil and the Rack escalated. Petty crimes were committed—cars broken into and vandalized. The city came in for another inspection and upped the violation total to sixty. The FBI kept a blue surveillance van down the block and harassed them with daily phone calls. On some, they played tapes of private conversations from inside the Rack. No one knew how they were getting them and a search for electronic bugs inside the room was fruitless.

On one such call, Red listened as Kilroy protested innocence. "We don't allow any gambling of any kind in here," he said. He cocked the phone partially off his ear so Red could hear the agent's reply.

"Oh yeah?" the agent challenged, "what about this?" He played a short piece of tape that sounded like Zedec offering an unrecognizable man the opportunity to play One-Pocket for a thousand a game.

Kilroy raised his eyes at Red before answering. "You're taking that shit out of context. They knew you were listening and tried to get your goat. Gil doesn't allow any gambling of any sort in here."

"You know we're not going away. We're gonna stay on your ass 'til you screw up or close up."

Kilroy got angry. "You can't do anything to anybody. What you gonna do? Put us all in jail?"

"We can."

"So what. You know what that means to me? Not a damn thing. It means three squares and a bed. It means I don't have to worry about where I'm gonna sleep or what I'm gonna eat."

"You won't like the food in a federal penitentiary."

"You don't know who you're talking to—I grew up on *lard* sandwiches—when we were lucky."

"Give yourself a break. Give up the big shots. We'll let you walk."

"There's nothing to give you. There's nothing going on here—no gamblin', no nothin'.'"

"Sure, there isn't."

Kilroy smiled at Red. "I'll tell you what," he joked with the agent. "I'll make it easy on you. I'll give you a key to the joint. You can come in any time you want, day or night, and see for yourself. This is strictly a law-abiding joint."

"Hang up on him," Red said. He made a motion of disgust and walked over to the closest pool table, picked up a cue stick that was lying there, and poked at a shot. When Kilroy got off the phone, he showed him a One-Pocket move Zedec had used the night before.

Red didn't think about the phone call again until Kilroy pulled him aside a few days later.

"Fucking FBI."

"What now?"

"They taped that conversation—you know—the one where I said I'd give them a key. They edited it so it sounded like I was working with them. They played it for Rat-Face."

"Oh, boy," Red sympathized.

A few weeks later, Kilroy's *mother got sick*, and he went back East to take care of her. A week later, Gil's physical condition deteriorated beyond the point of being able to manage a poolroom. He turned the Rack over to Zedec and another guy and retired to Miami with his wife.

Zedec proceeded to milk the Rack for everything he could. The repairs required by the city were blatantly ignored and the violation total soared to over eighty. The upkeep required to run a business from day to day was totally disregarded. Most of the time there wasn't even toilet paper in the john. Anybody who was not a regular, and didn't know any better, was shook down at the door for a *cover charge*, by whomever thought they could get away with it. Any semblance to a centralized, responsible management was gone and so were the "Millionaire Jews." All of the gambling action centered around Rubie, the only big shooter still coming around. He lost hundreds of thousands.

One day Red came in with a friend of his, to find the doors wide open and the place completely abandoned. They shot a game of pool while they waited to see who else would show up. After an hour, they got bored and left. Within days, the Rack was closed for good, its doors padlocked like those of the Hole over twenty years earlier. It was the end of an era. The heyday of big time stakes pool had come into the world, lived a full life, and had died.

For two years, the money was hard to come by. It seemed as if the more concern Red and Bernie had about it, the scarcer it became. It was as if Red had been working for one of the big automobile companies and had been unexpectedly laid off. They were accustomed to the flow of money from the prosperous years and it was hard to adjust. Red worked like hell to get a game and when he did, it was usually for small stakes. He moved all over town to pick up a little here and a little there. He kept his positive attitude as best as he could—he expected it to turn around for him, but it never did. The interest in pool was at the lowest he had ever seen. At one point, he even considered getting back into the carny games and went as far as looking up Tommie's phone number, before his mind revolted at the idea.

Five times Red went with Bernie to eastern Kentucky and ran booze with one of her brothers. Walker had been running alcohol from a neighboring wet county for years. Once, he was caught with an unbelievable nine-hundred and ninety-nine loose bottles of beer crammed into a Volkswagen Beetle. It made the front page of the county newspaper and made him famous.

It was after one of these bootlegging trips, in 1985, that Red got the bad news about his mother. She was ill and failing fast. By the time he made it to her bedside, she was already gone.

It was a shock of unbelievable proportion. Red had never even considered the possibility of Maurine dying. Even though he didn't see Thomas and his mother very often, they were always present with him—always there for him in some count-on-able way. Like the sun coming up in the morning. Like the ocean being there if you went to check on it. It was expected to be there—and so was Maurine.

Red fell into a deep depression. He was fifty-four and life made no sense. He had recurring urges to go to the phone and call his mother. He would be part way to the phone, sometimes with it even in his hand, before he remembered. Once, he had even dialed before he remembered. He would sit in front of the TV for hours, and not know what was going on when Bernie asked him. She would change the channel on him and he wouldn't even protest. Finally, she couldn't take it any more.

"You have to get out of the house, Bill. You're driving me nuts."

He looked at her, his face blank. "Where am I gonna go?" he asked.

"Beryl called about a poker game downriver—why don't you go there?"

There was no change in his expression. "I don't feel like playing poker, and I don't have any money to play with anyhow."

"I've got a little bit you can have, Bill." She left the room and returned a minute later with a small roll of bills. "Here. Take this and win us some more."

Red made no motion to get up from the couch, but neither did he resist when she grabbed him by the elbow and urged him to his feet. She got a light jacket from the closet, helped him put it on, and zipped it up. She watched from the front door as he got into the Buick and drove away.

Several hours later, the phone rang. It was Beryl.

"Cornbread's not feeling very well, Bernie."

"I know," she answered. "He's been upset ever since his mother died."

"No. I don't mean that. I mean physical. There's something wrong with him. He can't move his arm and he says he's numb all over."

"You better bring him home."

"We'll be there in twenty minutes."

She hung up the phone and went to the front window and looked out. It was dark now, with a light rain falling. She sat on the sofa and waited. When she heard the car pull into the driveway, she got up and went to the door. By the time she turned the dead bolt and opened it, Beryl was already standing there.

"Where's Red?" she asked.

"He's in the car, Bernie. He's bad off—I think we got to take him to the hospital."

She grabbed a coat and scarf. When she got to the car, Red was slouched in the front seat, on the passenger side. She got in the back and leaned over to see his face. It was white and cold to the touch. She directed Beryl to the hospital and within minutes, they were in the emergency room.

The admitting nurse took one look at Red, spoke quickly on the intercom, and led both he and Bernie to an inner room. They were met by another nurse and a doctor who quickly removed Red's clothes, medicated him for pain, and got him into a bed and hooked up to a couple of machines. A nurse took Bernie by the arm and led her to the waiting room and instructed her to remain there.

For the next twelve hours she fretted—pacing the floor, drinking coffee, and trying to read magazines. Finally, an aide came and led her into an examination room where she was introduced to two doctors. A few moments later, Red was wheeled in by a large nurse in a white starched uniform. He smiled weakly when he saw Bernie.

The nurse opened up the back of Red's hospital gown and pulled it down to his waist. One of the doctors assisted her as she placed a series of suction cups on his chest. The nurse flicked a switch and both doctors turned to look intently at a screen that was connected to the cups by a mass of wires. They relaxed as the image on the screen showed a regular pattern.

"That doesn't look too bad," one of them said. "Help him up and put him on the treadmill," he instructed the nurse.

Red got up, with her help, and walked to the other side of the room where he stepped onto the machine. His left shoulder was slumped and curled forward.

"All we want you to do here, sir, is to walk slowly. Just like you were taking a leisurely walk in the park. That's fine. That's good." The doctor speaking was looking back and forth from Red to the screen. The other doctor was writing on a form clamped to a clipboard.

"Let's pick up the pace a bit, sir," the doctor with Red said. "That's good. A little more. Fine. A little faster." He turned his head to look at the screen at the very second the machine erupted with a loud series of high-pitched sounds. "Whoa, whoa!" the doctor shouted. "Stop! Right now!" The line on the screen was wild and erratic—jumping without rhythm or pattern.

"What's going on?" Bernie cried out, but was pushed aside by the nurse as she rushed to Red. He was slumped over, his elbows on his knees. Both doctors were yelling at each other and at the nurse. She filled a syringe with a clear liquid and injected it into Red's forearm. Within seconds, he was taken away by two emergency workers, the nurse, and one of the doctors. The other doctor stayed in the room with Bernie.

"What's going on?" she cried again.

"Your husband needs to get back to the emergency room immediately," he answered.

"Why—why? What happened to him? What happened to my husband?"

"Your husband just had a massive heart attack, Mrs. Burge, and may very well require surgery. Are there any family members you'd like to call?" He led her to the waiting room and turned her over to a Red Cross volunteer.

◆   ◆   ◆

Red struggled to wake up. His mouth was incredibly dry. He tried to gather up some saliva, but could not. He could not remember where he was. He tried to speak, to cry out for water, but was unable. Faces seemed to swim in front of him. Some came in close, magnified and out of focus. He recognized none of them. Colors moved by his field of vision in big swirls—greens and blues. There was a brilliant yellow to his right that called to him, but he couldn't focus on it. It was too intense.

He gave up and closed his eyes. An incredible crushing pain permeated his entire being. It receded to his chest, paused there for a moment, and then hurtled to his head, his extremities, and beyond to the limits of consciousness. He tried to hide from it, to move from it, but there was no where to go. The unbearable thirst returned and he tried to cry out, but failed.

He became aware of the intense light again and struggled to open his eyes. With a great effort he forced himself to stay in its presence. There was a rending—a tearing—like that of an invisible membrane. It brought a tiny space of relief, and in that tiny space he felt a wetness—a minuscule flow of wetness under his eyes that was cool in the heat of the light. He couldn't tell what the wetness was, and struggled to keep his attention on it. As he let his breath out, the pain receded to his chest again, and the wetness moved out in front of him. He forced himself to look at it.

It was blood. Blood everywhere. It was on the blades of grass—the tall blades of grass swaying in the wind. Blood all over the edge of the concrete where the bridge met the path. A faint voice called to him from the direction of the yellow light, just behind him. He tried to turn—to respond to the voice calling him—but could not pull his eyes away from the crushed trail of bloody and matted grass in front of him. Then he saw it. Right there. Right there by the edge of the bridge. The eyes stared at him. The misshapen mouth with its swollen tongue leered at him.

He gasped for breath and the pain from his chest racked him and he almost blacked out. As he struggled to stay awake, he became aware of a presence—a shadow between him and the light. He heard the voice again—close and immediate.

"Red. Red. What is it? What is it for christsake?" It was Tommie.

In the moment of realization, there was a further ripping of the membrane. His eyes opened and his vision cleared. He was aware of the sunshine, the brilliant blue sky, and the bright green of the grass and the nearby wood line. He was aware of Tommie pressing against him as he, too, saw the severed head lying in the bloody grass. Red looked down at his exposed abdomen and was spellbound by the way it was undulating with continuous waves of physical emotion—rivulets of sweat rolling down to the bottom of his shirt where the last button was buttoned. He saw his dusty shoes, where he stood just inches from the dark brown stain in the dirt. A sound wrenched from his throat—a long, tortured moan, coming from a deeper place than even the hurtling pain which assaulted him again.

"Mr. Burge?" a gentle voice spoke. "Mr. Burge, are you all right?" The nurse wiped around his eyes with a damp, soothing wash rag. "You can have a drink now, Mr. Burge."

Red opened his eyes. He was in a small room with white walls. There was an IV stand with its hanging bag to his right. "Where am I?" he asked.

"You're in the recovery room," the nurse answered. "You've been out of surgery for about an hour now." She held a container with a plastic straw to his mouth. "Don't drink too fast," she said, as he drew in the cool, clean water. After a moment, she removed it from his mouth and set it on a metal table to his left. "I'm going to give you something for the pain," she said. He smelled rubbing alcohol and felt a tiny prick. In moments, the pain in his chest abated.

The nurse wiped his face again, and let him have another drink. "Are you a married man, Mr. Burge?" she asked, trying to draw him out.

He closed his eyes to remember and there was a jumble of moving images in front of him. There was a man with red hair as bright as his own, the sunlight gleaming from a razor in his hand. He tried to run, but his legs wouldn't move. The image of a woman, another redhead, came close and filled his view. She was comforting him, protecting him, reassuring him. It was Maurine. As soon as he recognized her, the image changed to Bernie's face. He let his breath out and opened his eyes.

"Yes," he said to the nurse.

"That's wonderful," she said. "And what kind of work do you do, Mr. Burge?"

It took him several moments to remember, but when he did, a smile of satisfaction reached his face. "I'm a pool player," he answered. "They call me Cornbread Red."

Epilogue

When Red got out of the hospital, the first thing he heard about was the new movie, "The Color of Money." Over the next few years, he watched with delight as the interest in pool intensified and the number of tournaments available for professionals increased dramatically.

He did his best to compete with the new players coming up, but it was tough. They were young, hungry, and eager to get to the top—he was tired and eager to get home and watch his grandchildren grow. While they were posing for photographs in the winner's circle, Red was posing with fans who knew him as *The Living Legend.*

Doctors found one of the sources of his fatigue—an aneurysm—and Red went into surgery again. They cut him from navel to groin, joining the surgical scars that ran from throat to navel to the ugly one on his thigh. Red had been opened up, over time, from top to bottom.

After a short recuperation, he entered the "Legends of One Pocket" tournament in Reno and came in second. It was an unbelievable repeat of the 1966 Johnston City World Championship. Once again, he battled it out with Ed Kelly to the last ball. Once again, Ed took the crown.

Red and Bernie sold the house and left Detroit. They retired to a quiet mountain top in eastern Kentucky—close to Bernie's family and miles from the nearest poolroom. Red lasted two months before returning to Detroit. He was last seen at one of his favorite haunts there—wolfing and haggling—boasting and bragging—daring someone to take a shot at him.

ATTENTION:
POOL PLAYERS!!!

THE "VIEW OF A CUE" POSTER IS NOW AVAILABLE FROM BEBOB PUBLISHING!

THIS 22" X 28" COLOR POSTER IS THE ORIGINAL CUEBALL REFERENCE GUIDE. IT WILL COMPLEMENT YOUR BILLIARD ROOM AND IMPROVE YOUR PLAY!

SEE THE FOLLOWING PAGE
TO ORDER YOURS
TODAY➡

ORDER FORM

Postal Orders: Bebob Publishing
PO Box 530411-A
Livonia, MI 48153

Credit Card Orders **ONLY:** (800) 879-4214

Wholesale Orders and Information: (313) 953-0363

Please rush: ☐ ## CORNBREAD RED
POOL'S GREATEST MONEY PLAYER

☐ "VIEW OF A CUE" POSTER

Name:_____

Address: _____

City:_____State:_____Zip:_____

Payment: ☐ Check ☐ Money Order **Total:** _____

You are entitled to a full refund of the purchase price if not completely satisfied, no questions asked. To receive a refund, ship item in <u>resaleable condition</u> to Bebob Publishing, PO Box 530411-A, Livonia MI 48153

Price: "Cornbread Red" (book): **$14.95**
"View of a Cue" (poster): **$14.95**
Shipping: **$3 first item & $1 each additional**
Michigan residents add 6% state sales tax
(Please allow four weeks for delivery)